Children on Brasses

BY JOHN PAGE-PHILLIPS

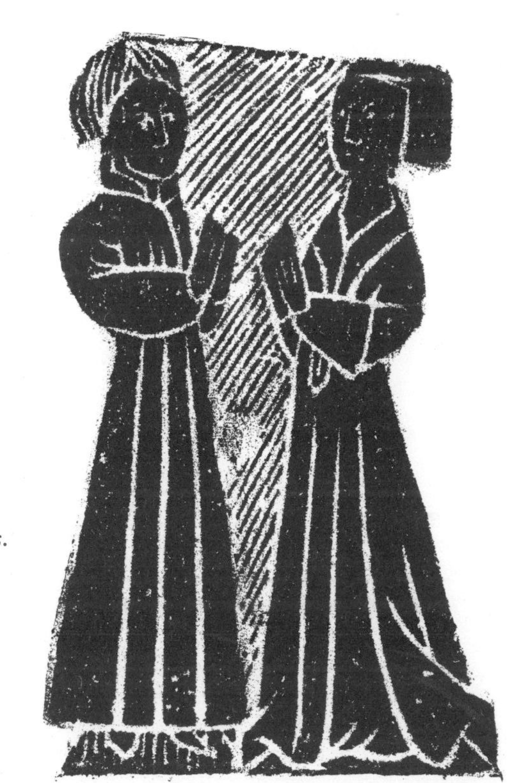

An unknown boy and girl (c. 1480), Peterborough Museum, Northants. Same scale. Rubbing (only) appropriated by the author for Livia and Benjamin his children, to whom this book is dedicated

LONDON · GEORGE ALLEN AND UNWIN LTD

First published in 1970

ISBN 0 04 739005 0

PRINTED IN GREAT BRITAIN BY JOLLY AND BARBER, RUGBY

Contents

Acknowledgements

I am indebted to Malcolm Norris for much initial help, to John Goodall, John Hopkins, George Kerr and Nicholas MacMichael. My wife deserves praise for her help with typing and editing. I am grateful to the City Art Gallery, Manchester, for Fig. 61, the Monumental Brass Society, for Figs 2, 4 and 42, the Society of Antiquaries, London, for Figs 1, 20 and 34 (part), and illustrations on pp. 11 and 19 and the National Portrait Gallery, London, for Fig. 22.

Illustrations

25. Daughters of Richard and Johane Yate, 1500, Longworth, Berks.
26. Five daughters of James Pekham, 1500, Wrotham, Kent
27. Eighteen children of Robert Baynard, 1501, Lacock, Wilts.
28. Children of Sir Thomas and Elizabeth Barnardiston, 1503, Great Coates, Lincs.
29. Swaddled babies John and Roger Yelverton, 1510, Rougham, Norfolk
30. Two children of Robert Heyward, 1509, Teynham, Kent
31. Anne à Wode and her twins, 1512, Blickling, Norfolk
32. Dorothy Parkinson and her twins, 1592, Haughton-le-Skerne, Durham
33. Nine children of John and Elyn Hampton, *c.* 1515, Mirchinhampton, Glos.
34. Twenty-four children by one mother, *c.* 1520, Burnham, Bucks.
35. William Bozard, 1505, Ditchingham, Norfolk
36. Margaret Aldriche, 1525, Yelverton, Norfolk
37. Wenefride Newport, 1551, Greystoke, Cumberland
38. Richard Newport, 1551, Greystoke, Cumberland
39. Group of sons, 1534, Radnage, Bucks.
40. Daughters of Sir Anthony Fitzherbert, 1538, Norbury, Derbyshire
41. Three sons and four daughters, *c.* 1550, Margaretting, Essex
42. Thirteen children on back of the figure of a lady, 1538, Okeover, Staffs.
43. Figure in furred gown, *c.* 1520, with smaller figure on back, *c.* 1540, Downing St. Museum, Cambridge
44. Twenty-four children of Peter Coryton, 1551, St. Mellion, Cornwall
45. Richard Best, 1587, Merstham, Surrey
46. Nathaniel Bacon, 1588, Aveley, Essex
47. Elizabeth Bacon, 1588, Aveley, Essex
48. Peter Best, 1587, Merstham, Surrey
49. William Brome, 1599, Holton, Oxon.
50. John Drake, 1623, Amersham, Bucks.

51. Thomas Tompkins, 1629, Llandinabo, Herefordshire
52. Twelve children of William Clerke, 1611, Wrotham, Kent
53. Anne Savage with her swaddled baby, 1605, Wormington, Glos.
54. Silvester with her twin sons and two other children, 1587, Lower Halling, Kent
55. Edward West, his wife and eight children, 1618, Marsworth, Bucks.
56. The infant William Hyde, *c.* 1630, St. Mary, Little Ilford, London, E.12.
57. Dorothy King, 1630, St. George's Chapel, Windsor, Berks.
58. Nine-month-old Arthur Wharton, 1642, Wooburn, Bucks.
59. Menelib Rainsford with his grandmother Anne Kenwellmersh, 1633, Henfield, Sussex
60. William King, 1633, St. George's Chapel, Windsor, Berks.
61. Memorial picture of Sir Thomas Aston and his dead wife, City Art Gallery, Manchester 2
62. Sons and daughters of Richard and Isabel Cheverton, 1631, Quethioc, Cornwall
63. Daughters of Nicholas Toke, 1680, Great Chart, Kent

Introduction

Although children on brasses are delightful, this is the first time that a book has been devoted to them. The text discusses their origins and traces the development of their designs. It is divided into two parts, the lesser-known and rarer examples of children on their own brasses, and the better-known groups on their parents' brasses.

Because these charming groups (or single figures) are small, they can be rubbed quickly. A detail (or small brass) rubbed in half an hour can give just as much pleasure as a huge rubbing that might take four to eight hours. They are also simpler to hang as decoration, or to store in a folder for study.

The county and chronological lists help one to find the brasses and the chapter on rubbing explains how you can make your own copy of the original.

Not all the brasses illustrated can be rubbed today. Some have disappeared, or rubbing is normally forbidden. 'N.R.' (no rubbing) indicates this in the lists at the end.

1. Children on their own Brasses

The Earliest Brasses

The earliest surviving brass in England is to Margaret, the little daughter of William de Valence (Henry III's half brother) who died in 1276. Although it is a 'brass' in that its design is a brass cross and inscription, there is no representation of the child – no hint of youth, no childish sentiment in the inscription. Her brother William died a year later and a similar brass is laid beside hers in Westminster Abbey. (They are now under temporary flooring and a step, so cannot be seen.)

The earliest actual representation of children surviving on a brass is nearly a century later – two children (*c.* 1360) at Sherborne St John (Fig. 1). The inscription, in French, reads 'Raulin Brocas and Margarete his sister lie here. God of his grace have mercy on their souls, Amen'. They are small half-length figures in close-buttoned dresses. The boy has short hair and cauliflower ears, the girl, long hair with a circle of flowers on top. Brasses in the thirteenth and fourteenth centuries were expensive and only the rich could afford them for their children. The rich parents of these two are not known, but the father might be Sir Bernard Brocas, a warrior (d. 1395) whose tomb with effigy lies in St Edmund's Chapel, Westminster Abbey. Perhaps the children succumbed to the bubonic plague that raged in the country in 1360–61.

At Great Marlow there was until 1832 a brass (*c.* 1388), to the four sons of Sir John and Dame Joan Salesbury (Fig. 2). They were shown as small kneeling figures looking up to a representation of the Resurrection. From their hands Latin prayer scrolls ascended. The brass was lost when workmen who were pulling down the church sold it as scrap metal. Fortunately dabbings or impressions of the children survive in the Society of Antiquaries and the British Museum, London.

A curious brass, from 1414, survives at Beddington (Fig. 8). At first glance it appears to be in memory of a mother and her many children. Thirteen small heads and shoulders are placed in a row beneath a full-length central figure. However, these are the brothers and sisters of the main figure, whose father, Nicholas Carreu, has his own huge brass alongside. He was M.P. and Sheriff at various times and his father had been keeper of the privy seal to Edward III. He could evidently afford expensive family brasses.

The Value of Children

The attitude towards children in medieval times was very different from today. Life was harder for them, and they lived at a time when England was endlessly involved in wars both at home and on the continent. Mothers, if they remained fertile, bore child after child with a high rate of miscarriage, death in childbirth and infant mortality. There were many diseases and repeated outbreaks of plague. Life was less highly valued and hopes were directed towards life after death. No monument showed this more clearly than the Great Marlow Resurrection brass. Children were begotten in quantity in order that a few might survive to be brought up. Their deaths were commonplace, and were less grieved over than the death of adults. Edward I, abroad on a crusade, hearing of the death of both his father and his son grieved more for his father, saying 'The loss . . . of children is easy as they can be multiplied every day; the death, however, of parents is irremediable because they can never be restored' (Rolls Series, Wm Rishanger, p.79). This lack of grief seems to have largely remained until Elizabethan and Jacobean times and few brasses or other memorials to children (who died young) were made before the sixteenth century.

Upbringing

Upper- or middle-class families might live in large households of thirty or forty people – parents, children, children's wives, grand-children, unmarried aunts, cousins, servants and apprentices. As the children grew to the ages of seven, eight or nine, both boys and girls were often sent away to the households of friends or relatives where they would remain in service for perhaps eight years. Sometimes a boy of good family became the ward of an abbot or began training to enter the church in a monastery (Figs. 9 and 20). A girl might be sent to a household with a view to marriage. Child marriages were sometimes arranged in order to secure property or settle a family feud. With high infant mortality a girl could have married three times before she was twelve. A 'superfluous' girl might be placed in a nunnery, either with a view to her becoming a nun (Fig. 28) or as a fee-paying pupil.

But girls' schools in nunneries never developed, because fees endangered the nuns' vows of personal poverty. On the other hand nunneries relied on the nuns to bring in wealth in some way for their continuance (Fig. 33).

The rich could pay for teachers, lay or ecclesiastical, for their children. But 'school' was not compulsory or free of charge, nor was it confined within the walls of cathedrals and monasteries. In the fifteenth century education developed more and more away from the Church. Fifteenth-century schoolmasters were sometimes married men.

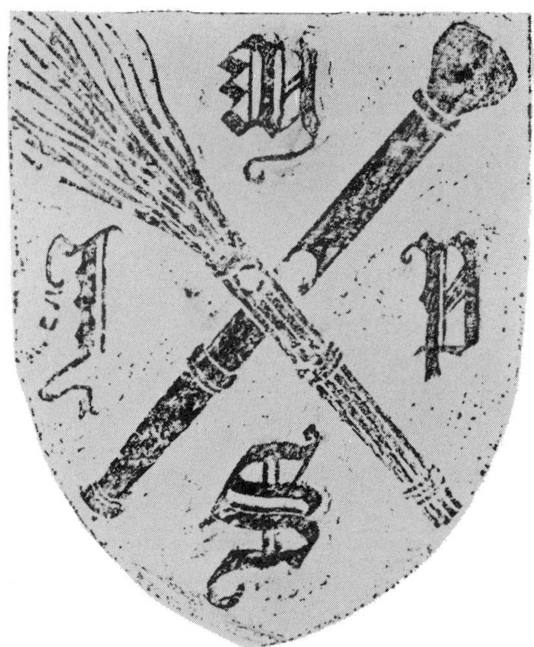

A birch and perhaps a palmer (for hitting the palm). A schoolmaster who died *c.* 1440 has reminders of his profession as his shield. Discovered at Denham, Bucks, on the back of a brass of 1545.

In a good household a boy might learn courtesy, music, heraldry, the orders of society, the use of weapons and how to carve at table. A girl might learn how to manage estates and servants, prepare food, drugs and clothing, and something about midwifery. The training, whatever it was, fitted the child for his or her place in society. Children of merchant-class parents were dependent for their education largely on the system of apprenticeship. Sons could not generally be apprenticed to their fathers so they went to friends' or relatives' families where they learned a trade.

Grammar schools and colleges multiplied in the fifteenth and sixteenth centuries. Evidence of Winchester school, built in 1394, is given by Fig. 16, and Eton, founded in 1440, by Fig. 18 (?). The alphabet and grammar were not learned without pain as the shield on this page suggests. It is associated with the figure of a friar (*c.* 1440) in gown and hood, his hands folded out of sight inside his sleeves. The initials I.P.M.S. possibly stand for 'Johannes Pyke *Magister Scolae*'. The rod was considered to be as necessary for children, both boys and girls (and often later for wives) as meat and drink.

Various brasses commemorate the founders of schools and colleges. Thomas Magnus founded a school in Newark (brass at Sessay, Yorks., 1550). Roger Lupton founded Sedburgh school (brass in Eton College Chapel, 1540). William Death founded the grammar school in Dartford (one of his wives is on the cover of this book) and John Lyon founded Harrow school (brass at Harrow, 1592). William of Wykeham and Henry VI as well as founding Winchester and Eton founded colleges at Oxford and Cambridge where boys could go at the age of about fourteen. Sir Nicholas Wadham (brass at Ilminster Somerset, 1609) founded a college at Oxford. At university boys learnt such subjects as arithmetic, logic, rhetoric, dialectic, music and astronomy, philosophy and theology. In order to study philosophy or theology boys had to be able to speak, read, and write Latin – often the abbreviated Latin found on brass inscriptions. Henry VIII was especially well educated and went to grammar school and university, studying rhetoric, dialectic, and music and learning French, Italian and Spanish. Ann Luke (d. 1538, brass at Cople, Beds.) was his 'norysthe' (nurse).

Dress

Childhood was brief and there was no separate world of childhood. Children were dressed and taught to behave like adults. A brass to a child often shows a figure which but for its scale might be mistaken for a grown up. In Fig. 35 at Ditchingham the son's gown and purse are very similar to the father's but only about half the size. At Holton (Fig. 49) a boy aged ten wears a doublet, cape and ruff like an adult. Girls are more easily recognized on brasses because they have long hair which advertises their unmarried state. Until recently it was a great occasion for a girl when her hair was formally put up. Of two girls with long hair at Etchingham, 1480, one has plaits. The mayor's daughter at Yelverton, Norfolk (Fig. 36), has hair below waist level.

Sentiment

One can see the beginning of a change in attitude towards children as early as the sixteenth century when brasses showing babies as at Rougham (1510, Fig. 29) or young children, as at Greystoke, 1551, and Aveling (1588, Figs. 46 and 47) begin to appear. By the seventeenth century both realism and sentiment on brasses to children become common. This is also evident on sculptured tombs like that by Maximilian Colt to Sophia, daughter of James I (Westminster Abbey). A baby sleeps in a life-size cradle and a Latin inscription describes her as 'a royal rosebud untimely plucked by death from her parents to bloom afresh in the rose garden of Christ'.

The sculptors and masons who made the alabaster monuments sometimes made brasses. Edward Marshall (1598–1675) was Master Mason to the Crown. He signed a brass of 1629 at East Sutton, Kent, and on stylistic grounds he may have engraved brasses showing babies in cradles (Figs. 57 and 60), a grandmother with her hand on her grandson's head (Fig. 59), and a little boy lying holding a rose, no doubt to bloom also in the rose garden of Christ (Fig. 58). These touching scenes demonstrate that parents are becoming more outwardly indulgent towards their children. But if a child is shown in a cradle or with a particularly chubby face (John Drake, Fig. 50) any gushing sentiment is kept in check by the intellectual conceits of contemporary metaphysical poetry. This is illustrated on the cradle brasses (Figs. 57 and 60) and perhaps most delightfully on the tiny pond brass at Llandinabo (Fig. 51).

2. Children on their Parents' Brasses

Origins – pedestals and arcades

The familar and delightful groups of children on brasses below or at the feet of their parents are not found in any established way before *c.* 1420. Their origin lies partly in the weepers of earlier sculptured tombs and brasses.

The canopy that arched above a sculptured altar tomb and the arcading on the sides of the tomb chest itself might have niches supporting prophets, angels, saints, or weepers. The more heavenly beings are generally placed in the canopy and the weepers or earthly mourners are more often placed round the tomb chest. The weepers are not necessarily specific people, but might represent important friends or relatives of the deceased. On John Eltham's (d. 1337) alabaster monument in Westminster Abbey, the weepers seem to include his parents Edward II and Queen Isabella.

The interpretation of this type of monument on a flat brass can be seen at Elsing, Norfolk, where eight weepers stand in the canopy on either side of Sir Hugh Hastings (1347). They can be described loosely as 'brother officers' whom he had fought alongside in France. They include Edward III. A drawing (Fig. 6) of the brass to Thomas of Woodstock (d. 1397), once in Westminster Abbey, shows a similar arrangement of weepers round a representation of the Trinity in a central shrine. The weepers are Thomas of Woodstock's parents and his eleven brothers and sisters. Of these, three died young, a sister Blanche, and two brothers, both called William. The brothers appear to be the two figures on pedestals and Blanche the only small female figure (although tall enough not to require a pedestal). The reason for the pedestals was to make short figures balance taller figures by raising them to more central positions in their niches.

The use of a pedestal for a child can be seen at Stoke Fleming (Fig. 4) where John Corp (d. 1391) stands beside his grand-daughter, Eleanor. By placing her on a pedestal her head is brought to the level of her grand-father's. At Cobham, Kent, a father (d. 1405) represented as a large figure in armour has two diminutive sons, (Fig. 5) on pedestals at his feet. The main pedestal has been inscribed in Latin 'Here lies . . .' with the son's names, and one concludes from the evidence from other brasses with pedestals that these were children who had died young.

Pedestals are not found on later brasses. Without them the relative ages (sizes) of the children are not always clear, and sometimes it is difficult to tell whether they were alive or dead when the brasses to their parents were made.

At Linwood (Fig. 7) seven children stand like tomb chest weepers in crenellated arcading below the main figures (1419). They are all of similar height. The Flemish-made brass to Roger Thornton (d. 1429) in All Saints, Newcastle-on-Tyne, shows fourteen children in arcading.

At Trotton a completely new arrangement appears, where a single son is superimposed as a small figure on his mother's dress (1421). This anticipates a change in design where children are placed in groups of sons and daughters at, or below, their parents' feet. There is an early example of this at Cobham, Kent, 1433 (Fig. 11) (wife of the knight with two pedestal sons Fig. 5) where six sons and four daughters stand with eyes raised towards their mother (1433). The same designer made the groups of four boys and twelve girls (in three rows) for a brass at Ashby St Ledger, Northants. (1416) shown on the back cover of this book. An arrangement on an early Norfolk school brass at Blickling (Fig. 12) groups the children in front of their parents, but all stare towards the viewer (1454). There are very many brasses designed like this and the inspiration probably stems from contemporary religious gift art—paintings, stained glass and embroideries. Fig. 3 shows an early donor mural painting (*c.* 1360) where the royal family gaze up at various New Testament scenes. They are separate figures each in his or her compartment, and so lack the bunching on Fig. 11.

Variety 1450 – 1500

There is wonderful variety in the groups of children that appear *c.* 1450–1500, and the draughtsmanship is generally good. Children at Broome, Norfolk (1455) and Longworth (Fig. 25) are dressed in shrouds. The sons at Stow-cum-Quy (Fig. 13) kneel in armour and wear tabards once bright with *gules* (1460). At Norbury there is a daughter (Fig. 46) wearing a tabard (the only daughter so dressed) (1538). At Elmdon (Fig. 20) one son (*c.* 1460) was dressed as an abbot holding a crozier. (The sons were stolen during the 1939–45 war, when slab and other parts of the brass were at Wendon Lofts). At Oakley one of four sons (Fig. 21) is dressed as a priest (1487). He became Archbishop of Canterbury in 1504 and a painting of him in a furred almuce hangs in the National Portrait Gallery, London (Fig. 22), attributed to Holbein. At Hinxworth (Fig. 10) each child is a small separate brass figure, and there is considerable variation in the heights. The tallest son wears a furred almuce. At Quethioc one son has a badge on his shoulder showing that he was a Yeoman of the Crown (Fig. 14). The marshalling of children beneath their respective mothers is shown clearly where a man had children by each of three wives (Figs. 15 and 23) at Thornton, and at Harrow. Some of the most attractive daughters are at Stoke Charity (Fig. 19) in berets or butterfly head-dresses.

Decadence (1500–1550)

Floor brasses were generally long and narrow, but many sixteenth-century brasses were placed on the wall above altar tombs to be viewed from the flank of the tomb chest, so that a lateral rather than a vertical design was more often used. Placing children to left or right of their parents assisted this, and followed more closely the donor grouping. The brass at Great Coates (Fig. 28) is an example. The children appear to have been an afterthought since they are on separate pieces of adjoining metal. At Beaumaris, Anglesey, on a wall brass (*c.* 1530) the children kneel behind their parents. Some deterioration in design can be seen, especially in London work of this period. The large groups at Lacock (Fig. 27, 1501) lack quality, and the twenty-four children at Burnham (Fig. 34, *c.* 1520) are boringly repetitive. This brass would tie with St Mellion (Fig. 44) for the record number of children by one wife which have been represented in brass, but the sons have now been lost so that St Mellion holds the record. The standard of engraving at St Mellion and the animated groups at Margaretting (Fig. 41) show great improvements on Burnham, but the temptation to make lazy re-use of old brasses, which were flooding the market after the dissolution of the monasteries in about 1540, led to some very awkward designs, the most horrific being that at Okeover (Fig. 42). At Teynham (Fig. 30) the same dull style as at Burnham has produced a remarkable juxtaposition of a swaddled baby and a daughter on one plate (1509). Compare this with the swaddled baby and boy, on separate plates (Figs 45 and 48) at Merstham (1587). Swaddled babies on brasses are often *chrysoms which means that they have died within roughly the first month of life. Examples are at Stoke d'Abernon, Surrey (1516), and Hornsey, Middx. (*c.* 1520).

*A cloth or chrysom was given to the child at baptism (the day of birth) and worn until the mother came to be 'churched' or purified by the priest. If the baby died during that time it was buried in the chrysom cloth and the name of the cloth thus transferred to the baby. Directions about chrysom cloths were removed from the 1552 prayer book.

Revival and Realism (*1550–1650*)

As a result of the Reformation pious inscriptions, saints and religious symbols were no longer decorative parts of brasses and heraldic and genealogical paraphernalia took their place. Parish registers of birth were introduced in 1538. Children on brasses are less weepers than part of an accurate genealogical record. A brass at All Saints, Maidstone, Kent (1593), shows Thomas Beale kneeling with his two wives and eight children. Above their heads are six tiers showing his ancestors similarly arranged and tracing his family tree back to the fourteenth century.

Death of the mother in childbirth is recorded on several brasses and the babies who either died with the mother or survived her are sometimes shown. At Blickling, (Fig. 31, 1512), and Haughton-le-Skerne (Fig. 32, 1592) a mother holds twin swaddled babies in her arms. A few late sixteenth- or early seventeenth-century brasses show a mother in bed. At Lower Halling (Fig. 54, 1587) twin babies are shown peeping from a cradle beside the mother's bed. The brass was eventually placed in her memory by the surviving twins. At Wormington (Fig. 53) one baby lies on the bed, and at St Cross, Holywell, Oxford, a lightly engraved scene shows a mother in bed, surrounded by three shrouded babies and one swaddled baby. The mother 'dangerously escaping death at three severall travells in childe-bed died together with the fourth' aged thirty-five in 1622. Memorial pictures may have been the inspiration for the design of these death-bed brasses (Fig. 61), where Sir Thomas Aston stands by a draped cradle and four-poster bed, in which his wife lies.

A brass at Marsworth (Fig. 55, 1518) shows mother and children grouped round the father's death bed, on which he lies in armour. The emotion of the family, where one daughter hides her grief in her hand, seems to come from direct observation and in that respect the plate breaks away from the tradition of praying hands. It is signed by Evesham, a talented sculptor, who conveyed a similar scene in marble at Lynsted, Kent (1518).

Three little daughters survive from a brass to Nicholas Toke, at Great Chart (Fig. 63, 1680). He is said to have survived five wives and walked to London at the age of ninety-three to find another, but died before finding her. Each daughter kneels on a cushion holding a book in one hand and a flower or branch in the other.

3. How to Rub Children on Brasses

Selection

You may wish to choose a brass to rub from the list in this book but it is only selective and there are many other children on brasses to be found. The only way of looking up *children* in a book (apart from this one) is from a list in *A Manual of Monumental Brasses*, 1861, by Herbert Haines or, more reliably, in *A List of Monumental Brasses in the British Isles*, 1926, (Appendix 1938) by Mill Stephenson (both available in the form of reprints). Many other books on brasses have general lists but they do not particularize about children.

Permission

No one may go into a church and take a rubbing without first obtaining permission. Crockford's *Clerical Directory* is the only single-printed volume for tracing Church of England parsons, and can be found in any good reference library. If you turn towards the end where the churches are listed you will find, reading across the page, the name of the incumbent. Under his name in the main body of the book, you will find his address and telephone number. If you are writing, a stamped addressed envelope should be sent for a reply. A fixed or voluntary fee is often charged for rubbing.

Equipment

There are only three essentials—*heelball* to rub with, *paper* to rub on, and *masking tape* to secure the paper while you rub. Old textbooks talk about using weights or hassocks to hold down the paper, but masking tape is much better. The paper can be securely held by tape at about 4-inch intervals, on the wall as well as on the floor.

All necessary equipment and advice on brass rubbing can be obtained from Phillips and Page, a shop at 50

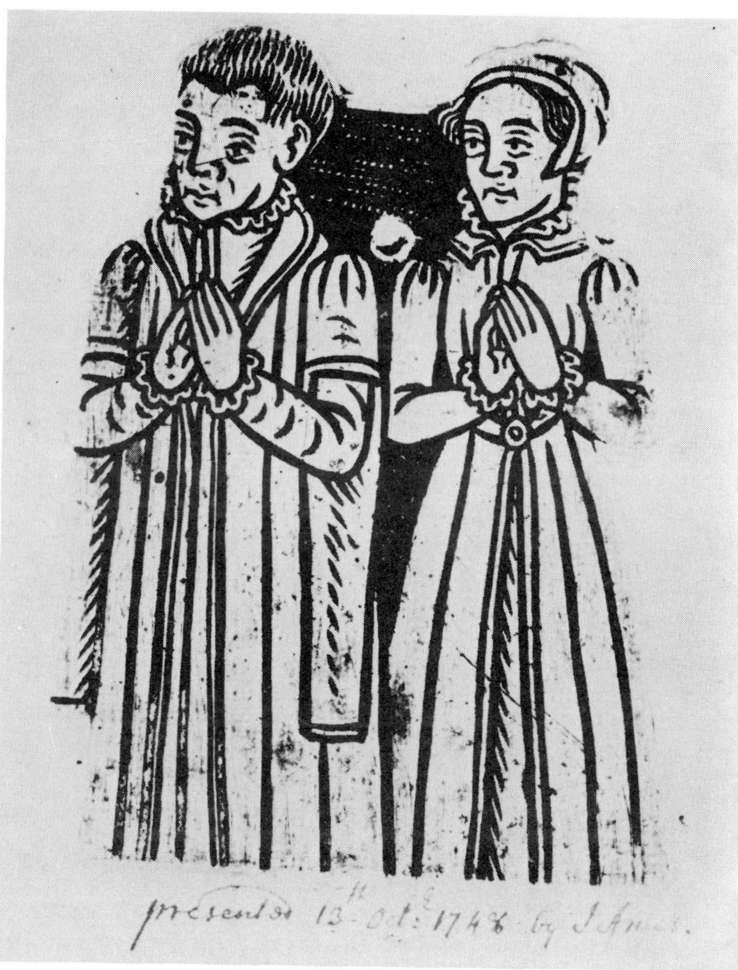

Kensington Church Street, London W.8. Equipment can be sent by mail order and a price list is available giving postage charges. A number of stationery shops also stock suitable materials.

The heelball you use should be sufficiently hard, so that there is no pile-up of wax on the paper in the lines of engraving, which would result in loss of clarity. It should also be heavily pigmented so that the colour, if black for example is jet black and not grey. The paper should be thin yet tough enough to transmit the image without loss of detail. If the rubbing is to be displayed or folded afterwards the paper should not be the kind that goes yellow or brittle with age. Paper is measured by the number of grammes in weight per square metre. 70 g.s.m. *all rag* paper is the best weight, and fibrous rag content gives more strength than non-rag paper. Paper, e.g. cartridge paper, over 80 g.s.m. tends to be too thick and paper under 45 g.s.m. tears

Left
Before brassrubbing with heelball developed in the 1840s direct copies of brasses were sometimes taken by inking a brass and using it like a printing block. The result was a looking-glass impression, unsuitable for recording inscriptions. This impression of children (*c.* 1560), whose whereabouts are unknown, bears the date 1748.
Society of Antiquaries, London. Reproduced full scale.

too easily. Shelf or wall lining paper tends to go yellow. Semi-transparent papers (e.g. greaseproof paper) with high size content become brittle with age.

Rubbing

1) Cut off sufficient paper from the roll to cover the area that you wish to rub. Children on brasses require very little paper.
2) Brush or wipe the brass with a soft brush or duster (handkerchief?) to remove all traces of grit and dirt. Check the surface with your hand to make sure that it is grit-free.
3) Stick the paper down at the corners, and at intervals, with short lengths of masking tape. Take great care not to dirty the wall. Make sure that the paper is flat and under even tension all over. If the screw heads on the brass prevent this, you can at this stage, break the paper round them with your finger-nail, and re-tension the tape.
4) Feel where the brass area lies and rub the first section lightly so that you pick up the edge, then rub *hard* in any convenient direction to get an even finish. Take care not to go over the edge as there is no completely satisfactory eraser. Then do the next section. It is wise not to attempt large areas at once. For rubbing children a 'stick' of heelball is more convenient than a 'cake' (which is a larger lump that can be held with both hands for large brasses). It is wise to hold your stick so that only a small area is rubbing on the paper (i.e. the corners or edges). A stick of heelball need never be sharpened like a pencil but can be turned in the hand to vary where it wears down.
5) When the rubbing is complete polish it lightly with a clean duster, cloth, or old nylon stocking – just as you would after waxing a pair of shoes – and peel off the masking tape. No fixative is needed on the rubbing if proper brassrubbing heelball has been used.
6) It is wise to note on each rubbing where and when it was made – it may be difficult to remember later.
7) Groups of children are small and can be cut out and stuck into an album, or on to cardboard with a mount, and framed like a picture. Wall-paper glues can be used, but a non-water-based glue may be preferred. An aerosol glue is easy to apply. Do not apply heat to seal the front or glue the back of a rubbing as you may melt the wax.

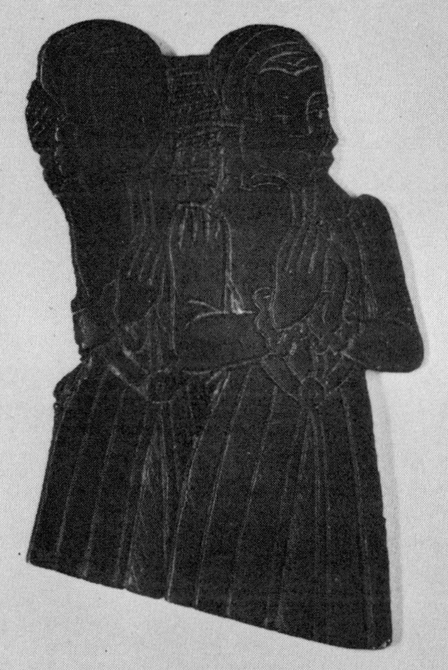

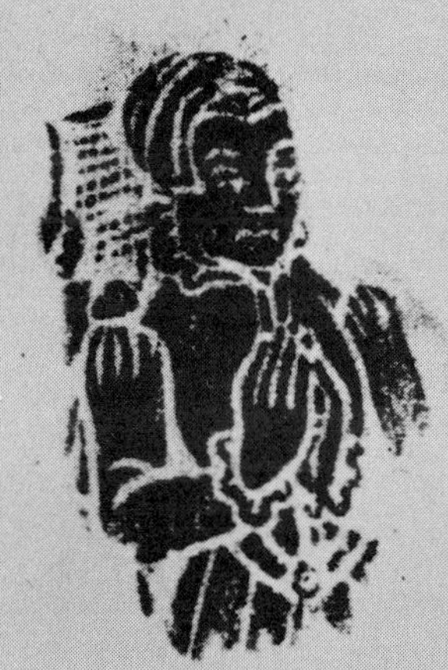

A group of two daughters *c.* 1560. The partial rubbing shows how heelball interprets the original engraving. Same scale. Recorded in Mill Stephenson's '*List of Monumental Brasses in the British Isles*', 1926, p. 589, under Derelict II Children (8), as 'Formerly in the Crisp collection', sold in 1922, lot 68. In the possession of the author since 1966.

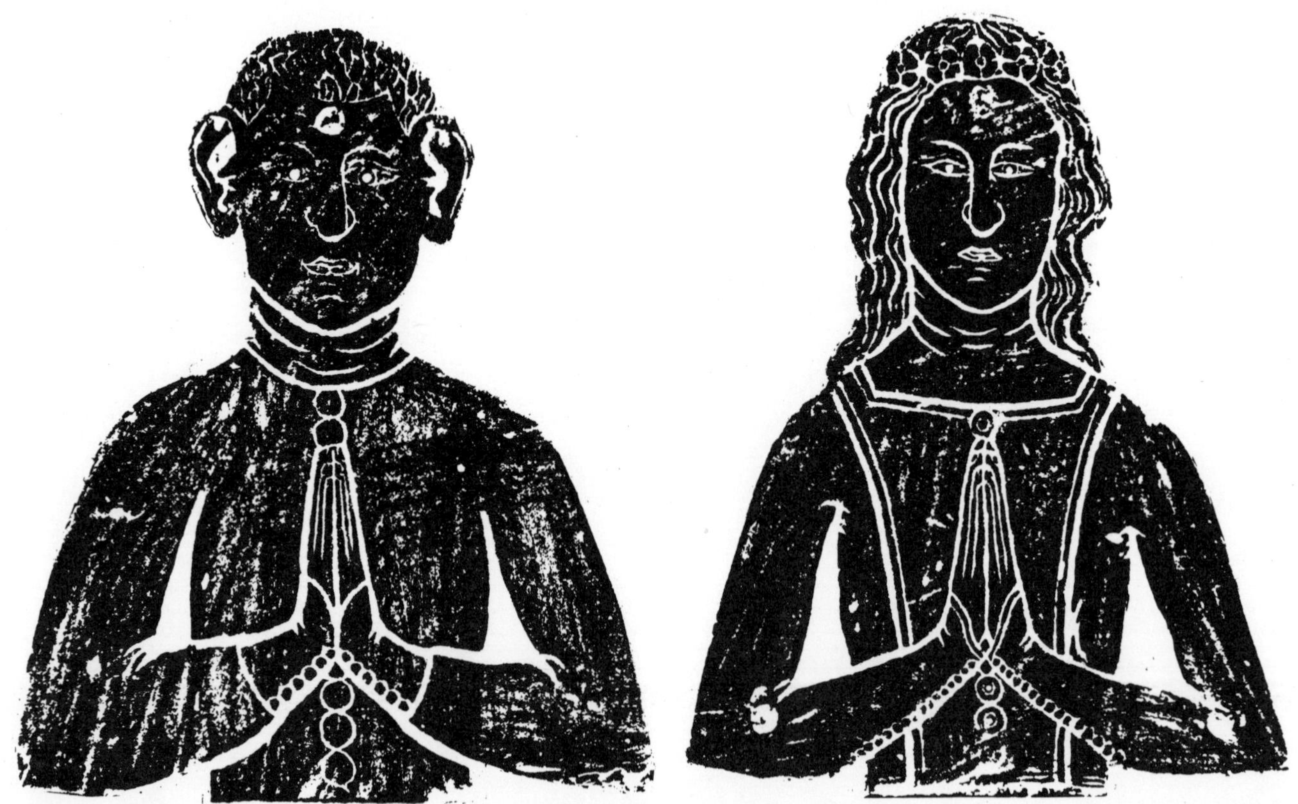

Fig. 1

Only rich parents could indulge in brasses for their children. The French inscription says: 'Raulin Brocas and Margarete his sister lie here, God of his grace have mercy on their souls, Amen'. Their father may have been Sir Bernard Brocas (1330–1395), whose effigy lies in Westminster Abbey. A famous soldier, he fought at Poitiers, Crecy (?), and Najara, and was M.P. for Hampshire and Chamberlaine to Richard II's Queen, Anne of Bohemia. Children engraved *c.* 1360. On wall of north chancel, Sherborne St John, Hants. Height $6\frac{3}{4}$ inches.

Fig. 2

The four sons (1383 and 1388) of Sir John Salesbury kneel below a representation of the Resurrection. Their father was esquire to Edward III, and later a firm supporter of Richard II, but was impeached with other knights who supported Richard, by the Parliament of 1388, and hanged. His fate was largely due to Thomas of Woodstock (Fig. 6) who headed the opposition to Richard. This brass was probably ordered by Dame Joan, their mother. It was lost in 1832 from Great Marlow, Bucks. Width of sons approx. 27 inches.

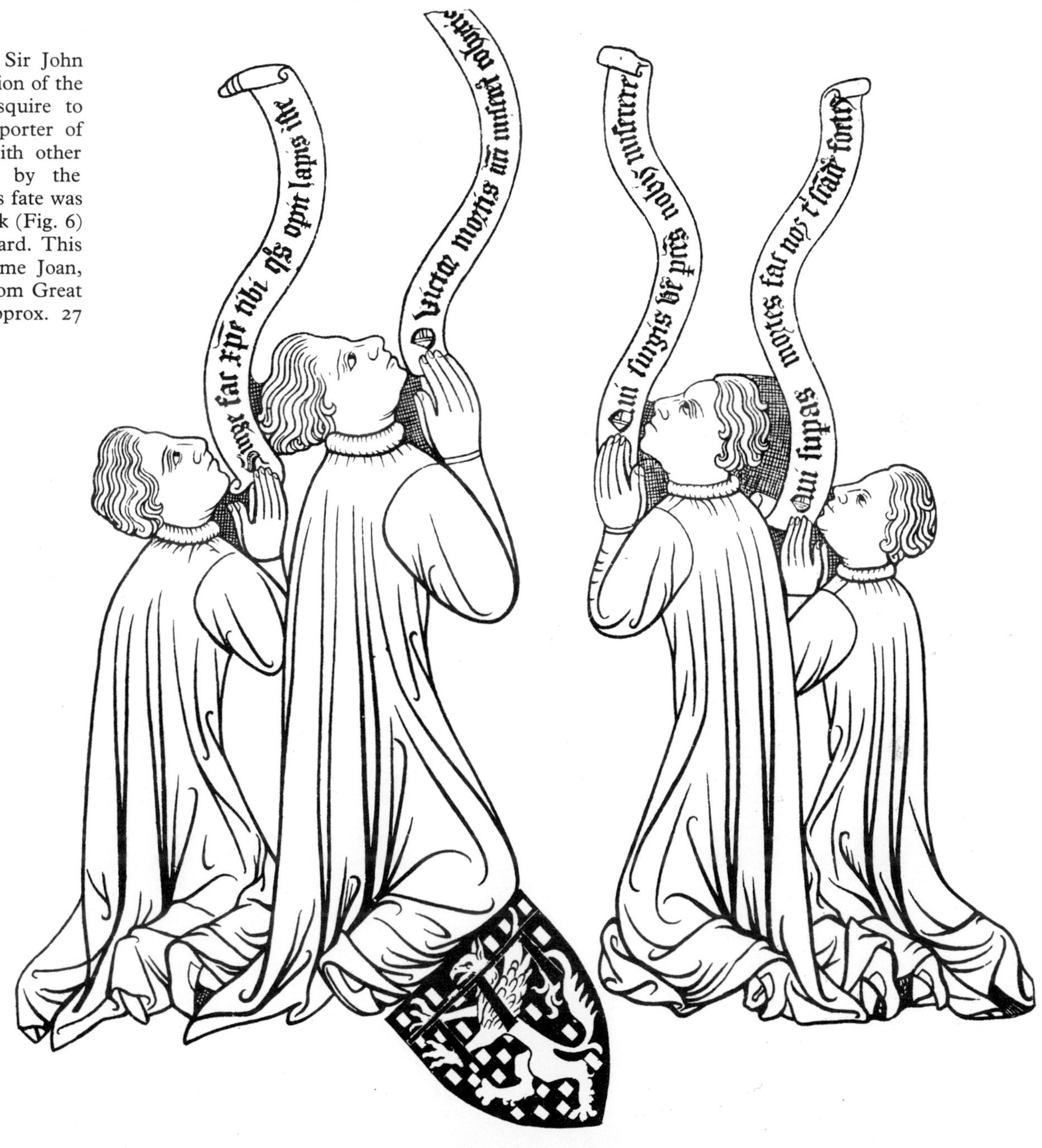

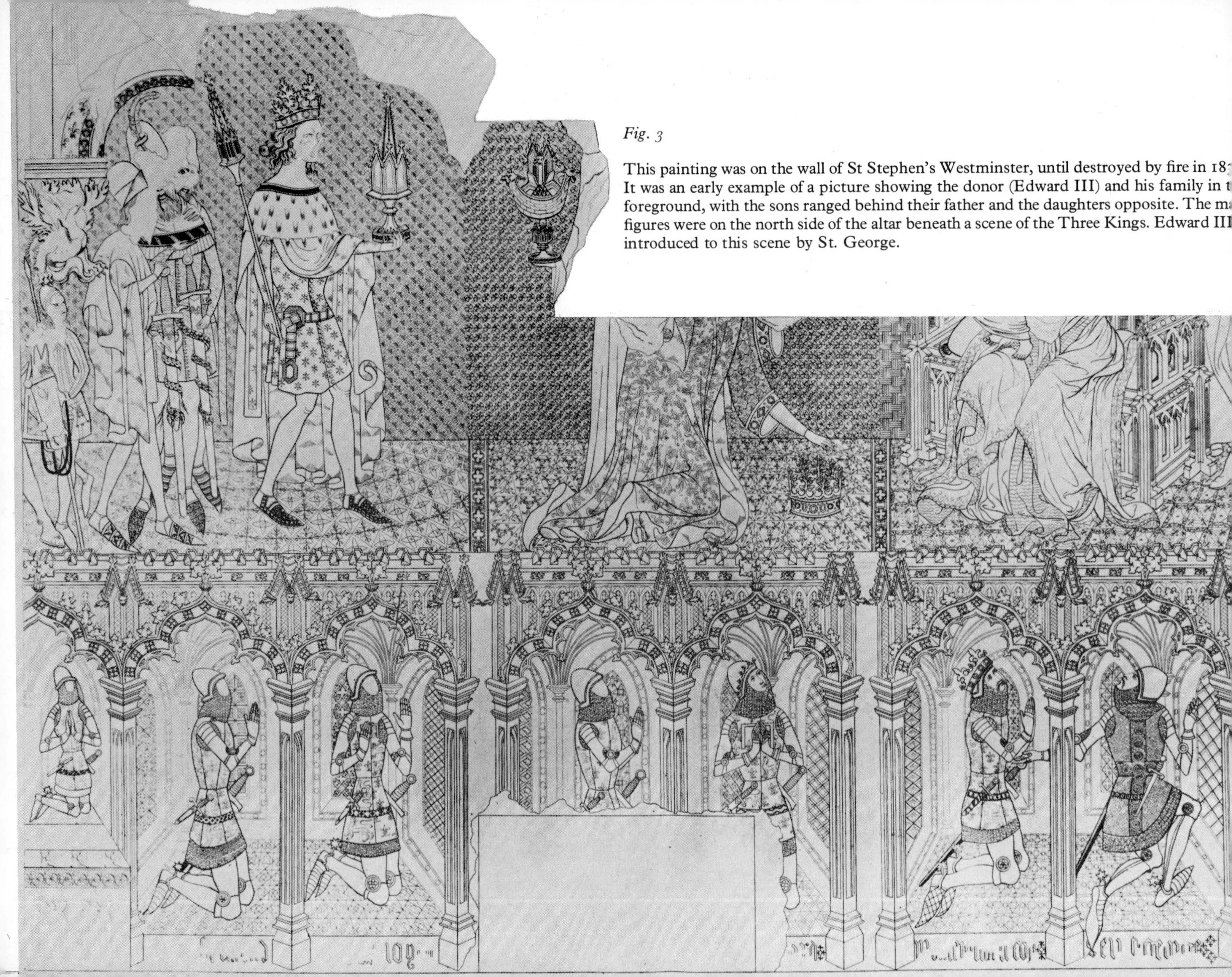

Fig. 3

This painting was on the wall of St Stephen's Westminster, until destroyed by fire in 18
It was an early example of a picture showing the donor (Edward III) and his family in t
foreground, with the sons ranged behind their father and the daughters opposite. The m
figures were on the north side of the altar beneath a scene of the Three Kings. Edward III
introduced to this scene by St. George.

The female figures were on the south side of the altar beneath the Presentation at the Temple, the Three Shepherds at the Crib, and a narrow scene of the angel(s) appearing to the shepherd(s). On later donor pictures the donor and his family were often placed in the main scene. The small son on the raised tile floor is Thomas of Woodstock (b. 1355) who would have been a child when the picture was painted (*c.* 1360). Such donor pictures may well have inspired the grouping of children on their parents' brasses in the manner of Fig. 11.

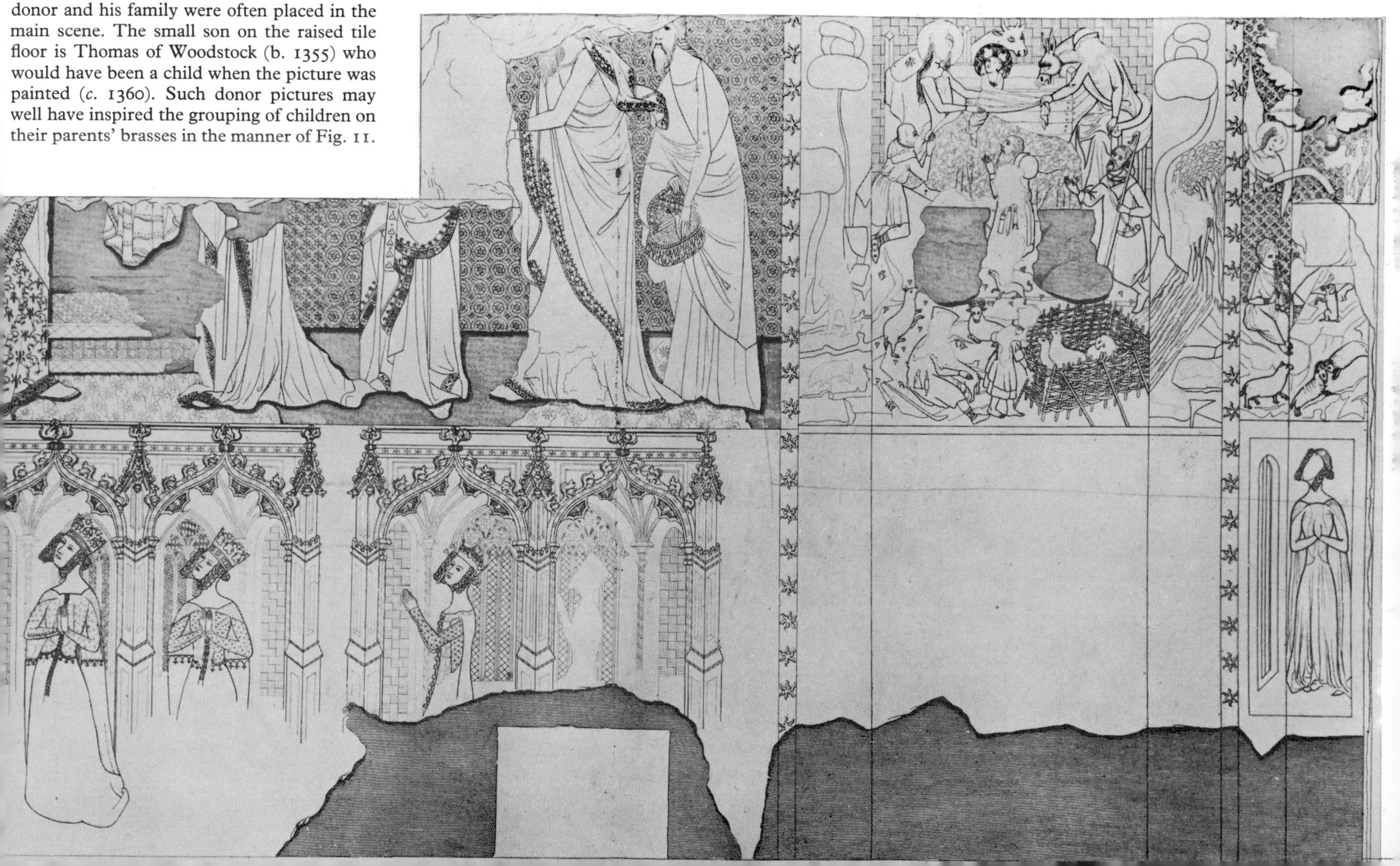

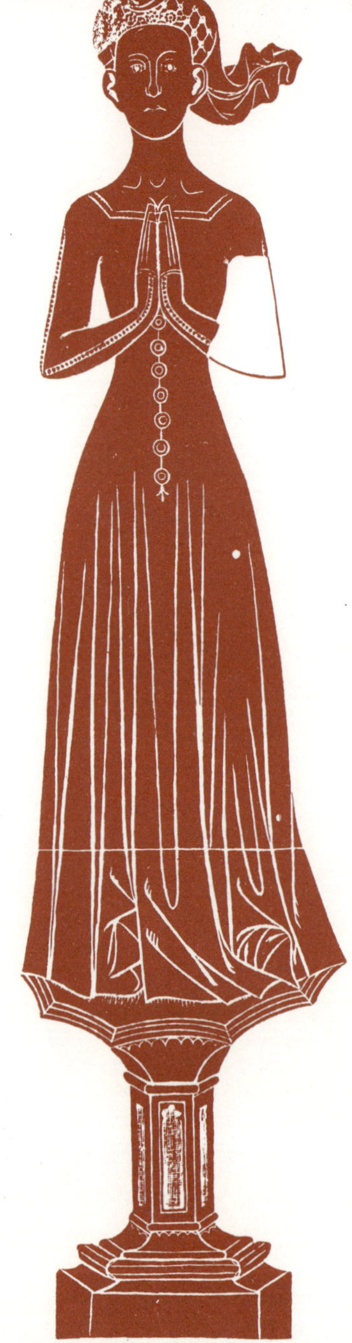

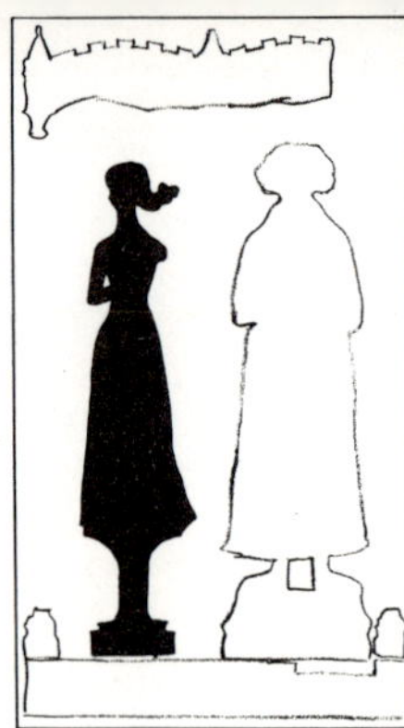

Fig. 4

A pedestal shows the youth of the child at death. Eleanor (d. 1391) stands on a pedestal that raises her to a level with her grandfather John Corp (d. 1361) beside her. These dates mean that there could never have been any grandparent – grandchild relationship, as there was, no doubt, in Fig. 59.

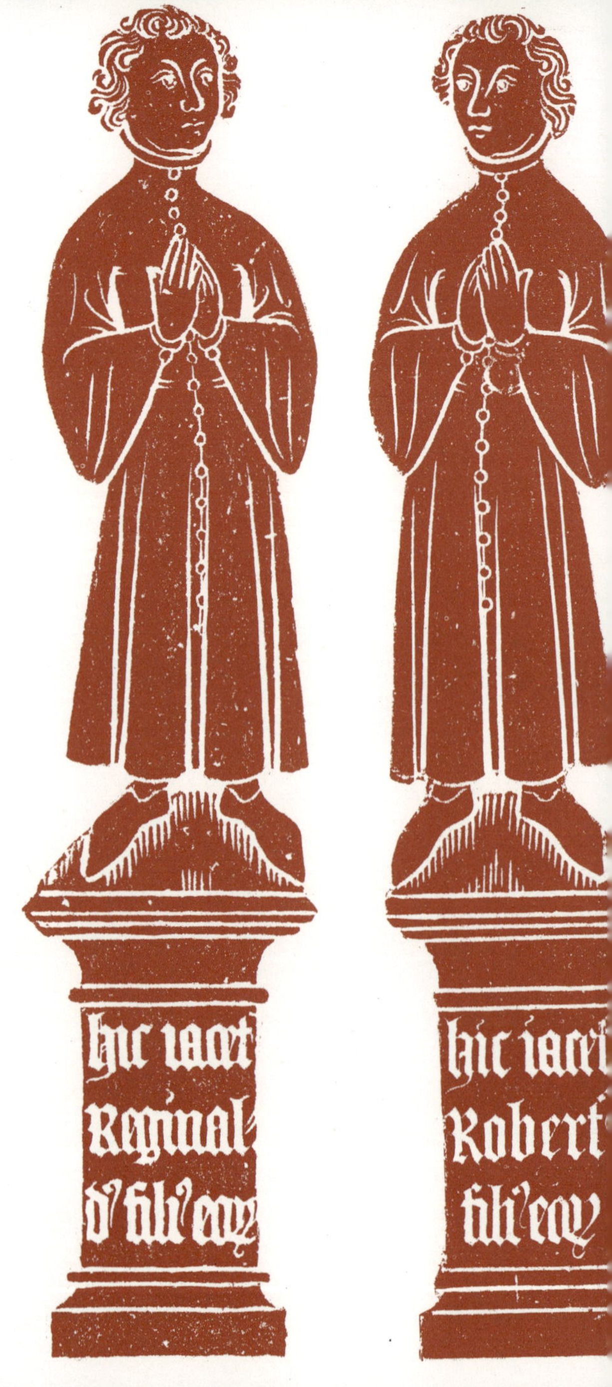

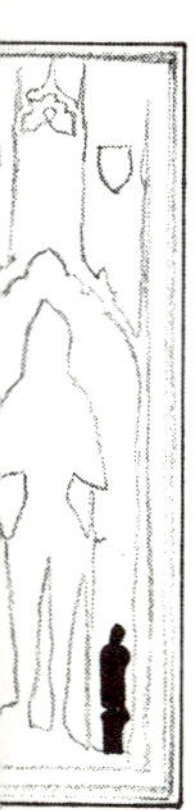

Fig. 5, left facing

These two young children Reginald and Robert, each 11 inches high, stand on pedestals on either side of their father, Sir Reginald Braybrook, who died in Middleburg, Flanders, in 1404. His is a life-size figure in armour, chancel floor, Cobham, Kent. The Cobham brasses (about 20 survive) have been much restored, but they form the finest single collection in the country. The figure of Robert has been renewed.

Fig. 6, right

The lost brass to Thomas of Woodstock (d. 1397). His parents, wife, six brothers and five sisters are ranged like mourners round the circumference, with Thomas and a representation of the Trinity enshrined in the centre. He was the seventh and youngest son of Edward III who is seated in the centre at the top. His mother Philippa of Hainault is on Edward's left. Two of his brothers are on pedestals and a sister is shown as a small girl. These must be William of Hatfield who died in boyhood, William of Windsor who died in infancy, and Blanche of the Tower who also died in infancy. Thomas was Earl of Buckingham and Duke of Gloucester, and married Eleanor de Bohun, whose brass is the finest surviving in Westminster Abbey. At times Thomas virtually ruled the country in opposition to Richard II until arrested and, according to tradition, smothered under a feather mattress. Only the grey marble slab survives in St Edmund's Chapel, Westminster Abbey. Drawing from F. Sandford's *Genealogical History of the Kings and Queens of England*, 1677.

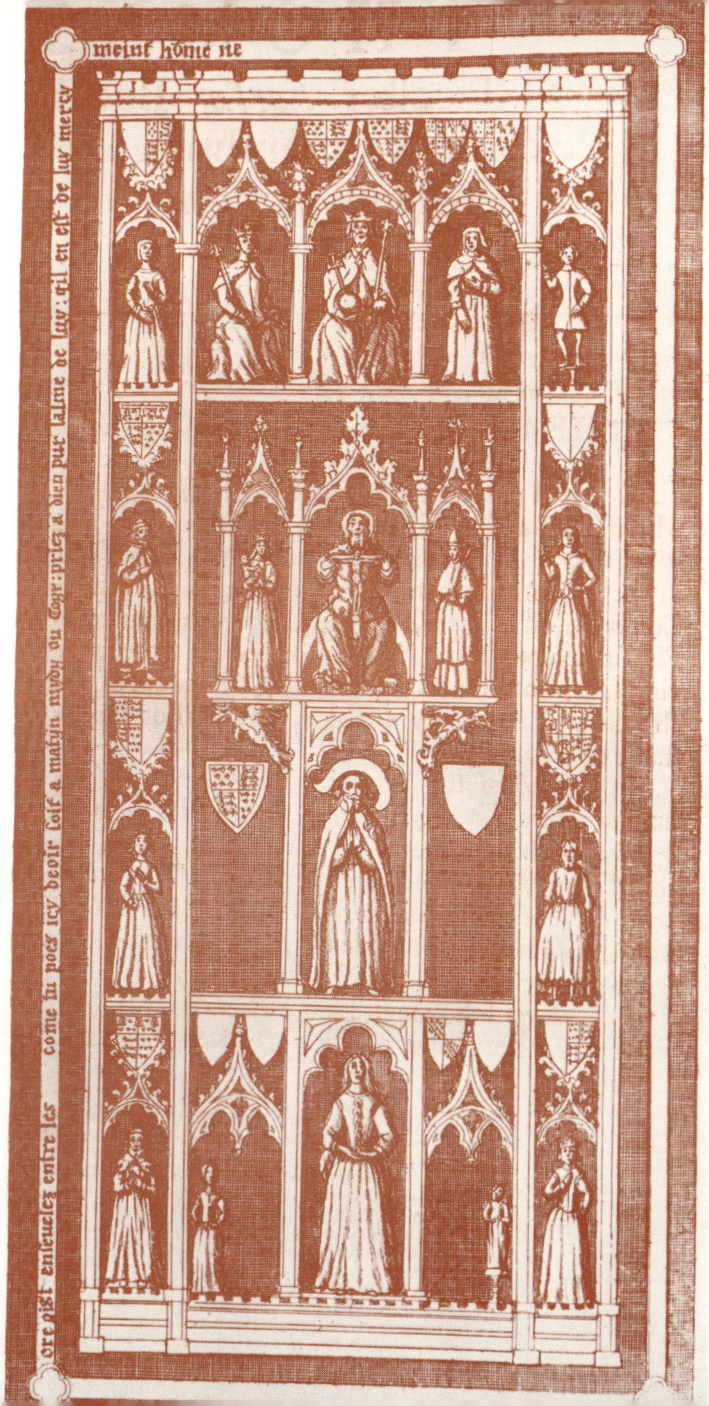

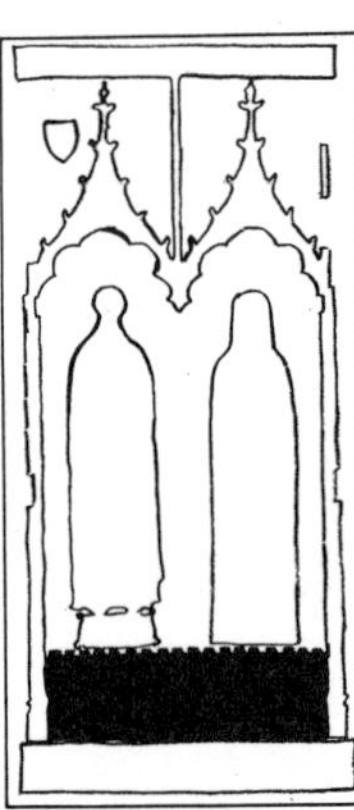

Fig 7

At Linwood, Lincs., the children of John Lyndewood (d. 1419) stand in crenellated arcading below the figures of their parents. The brass, worn by th passage of feet, is on the floor of the north aisle. John Lyndewood was a woolman and stands on a wool sack. The central son, William, in a long cassock became Bishop of St David's and author of *Provinciale,* the principal authority for English canon law. Width of arcade 22 inches.

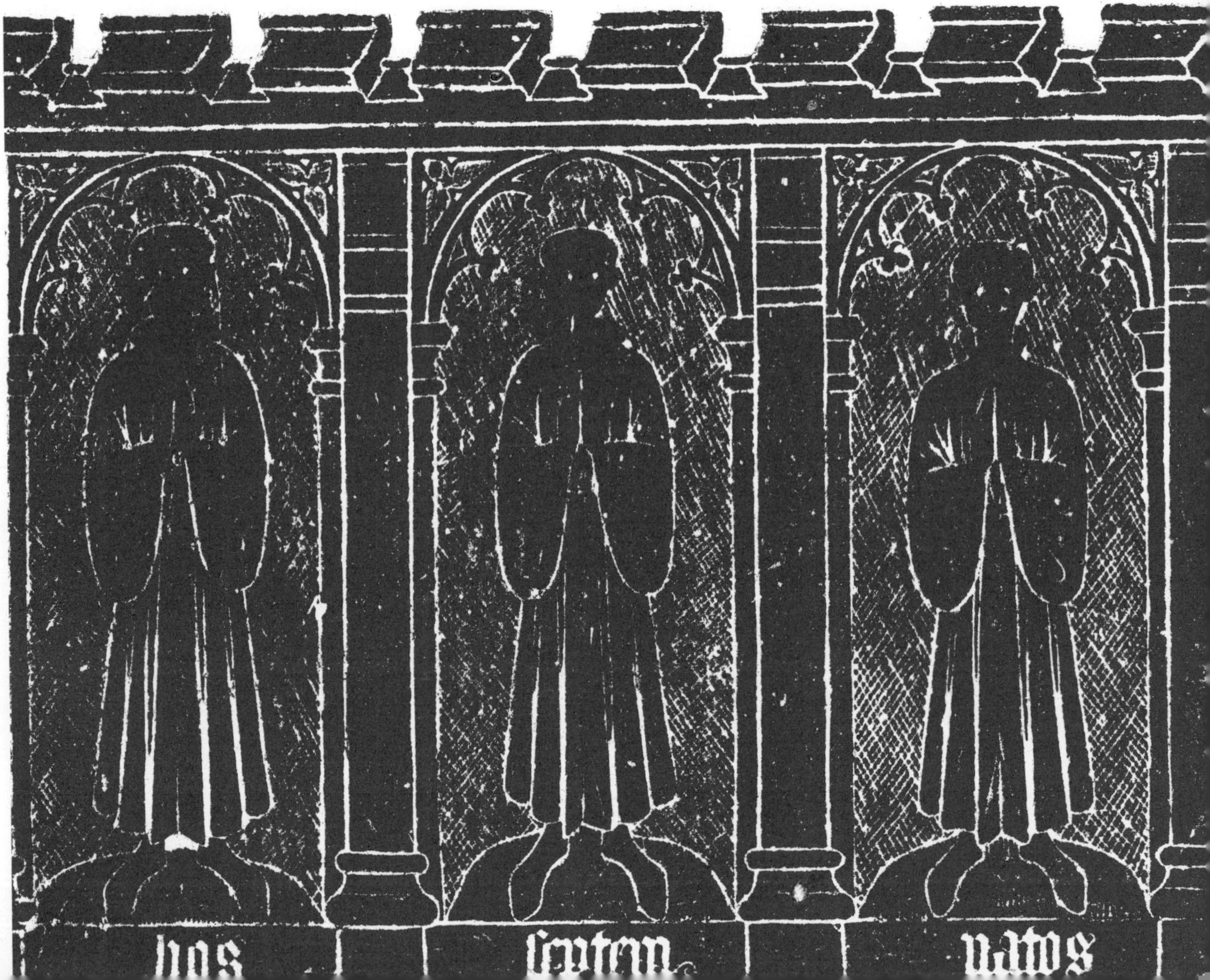

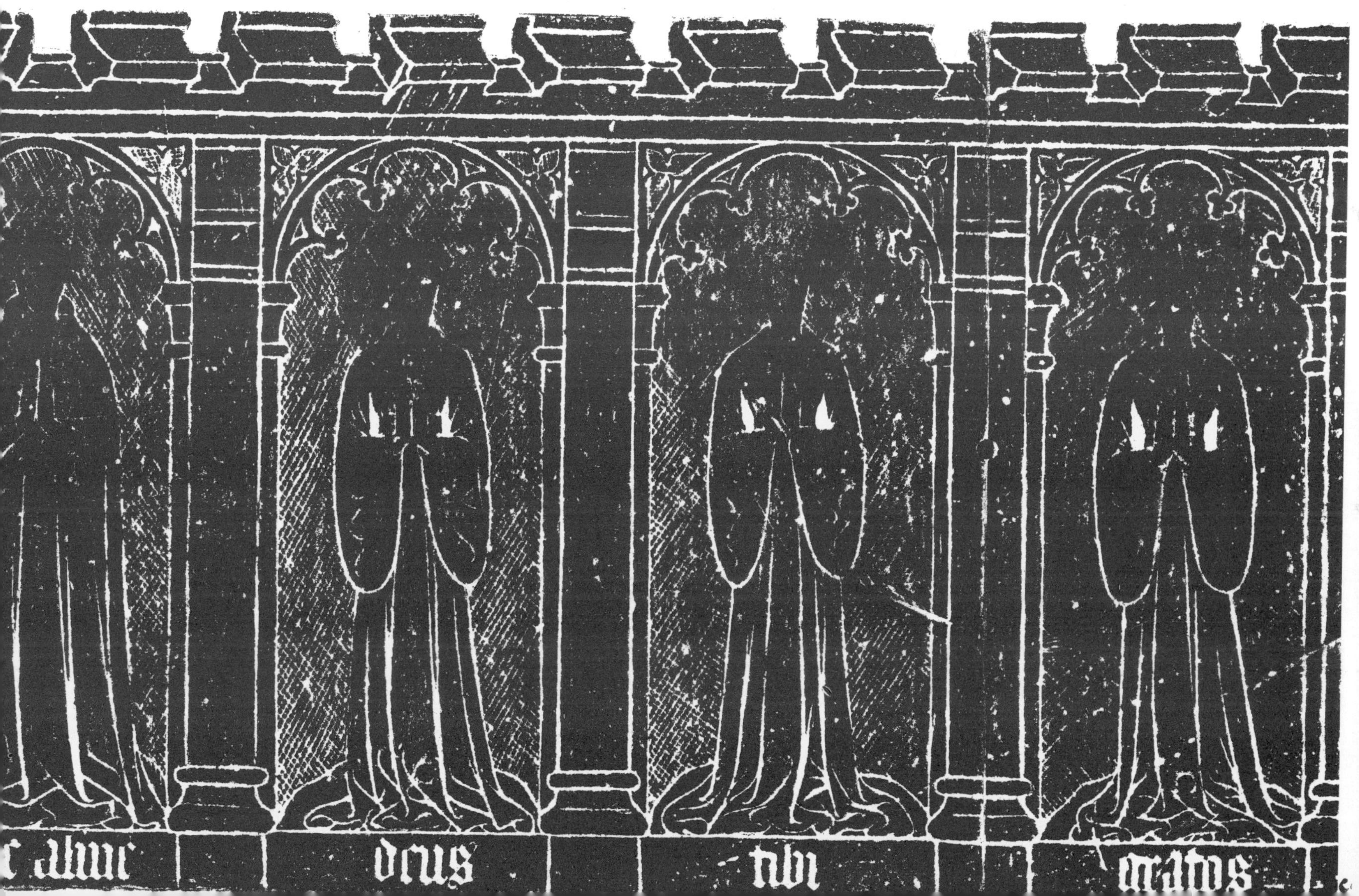
deus
tibi

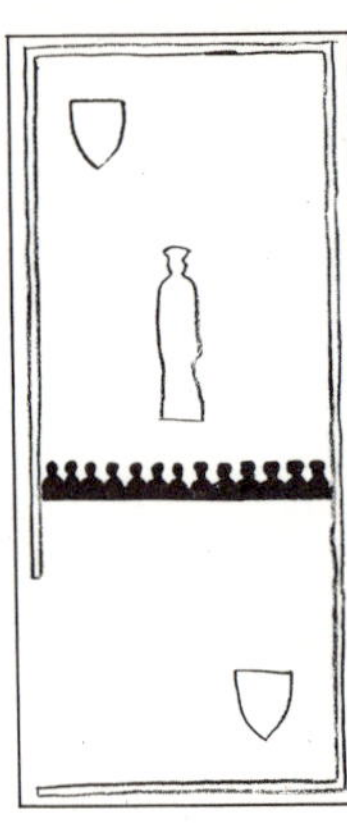

Fig. 8

The main figure on this brass is Philipe Carrue (d. 1414), and this frieze of children are her seven brothers and six sisters. Each child is named: there are four Johns, two Williams and two Agneses, suggesting that some lived very short lives. Occasionally parents did give more than one living child the same name. Floor of choir, Beddington, Surrey. Width of frieze 28 inches.

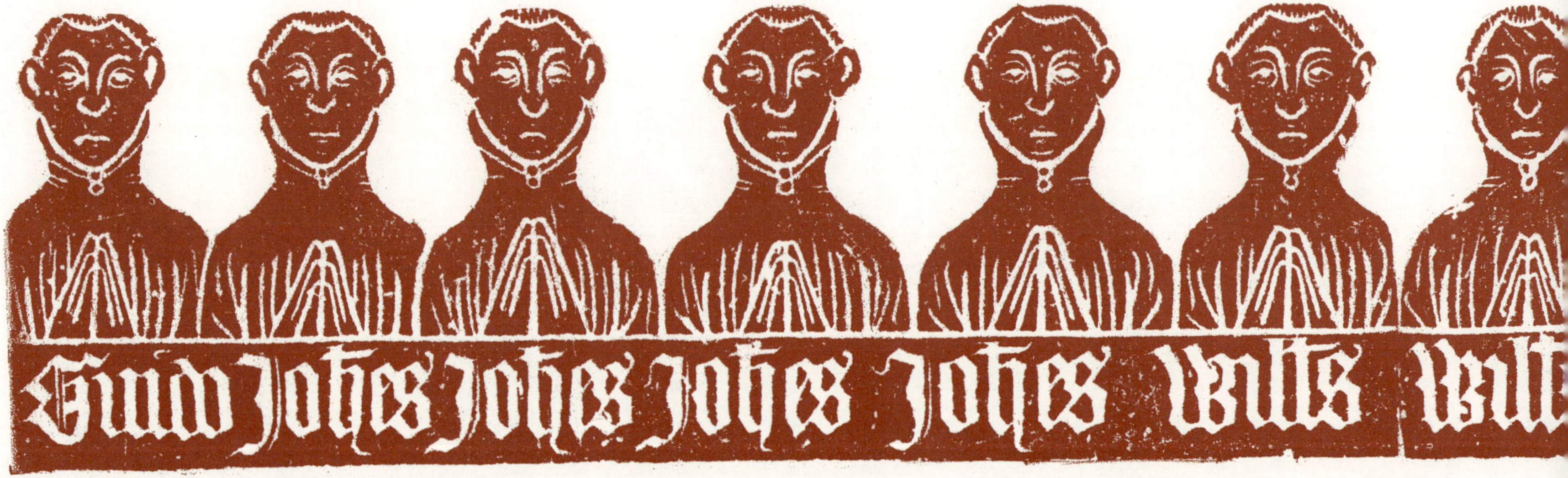

Fig. 9, over

These are the children of William West and his wife Joan (d. 1415). As their father had died 25 years before it seems that only the three larger figures were alive in 1415; they are the only children named in the inscription. They are: John, a chaplain, in albe and crossed stole, William, a marbler, and Alice (head lost). Now on wall beside their parents, north transept, Sudborough, Northants. Width 10½ inches.

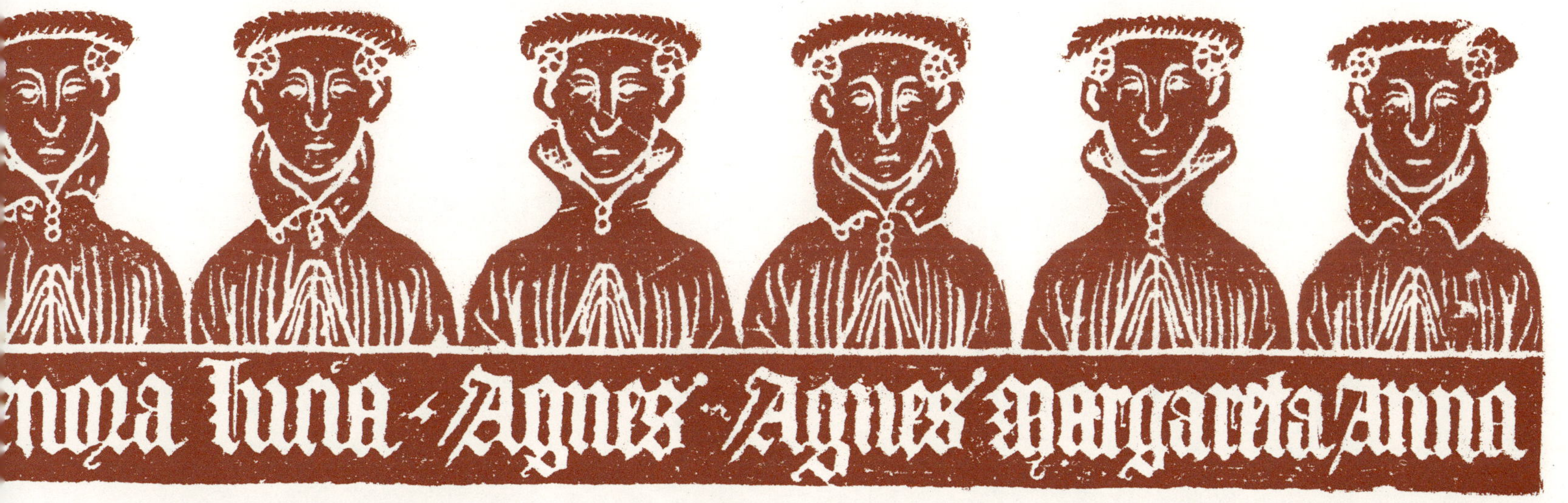

Fig. 9

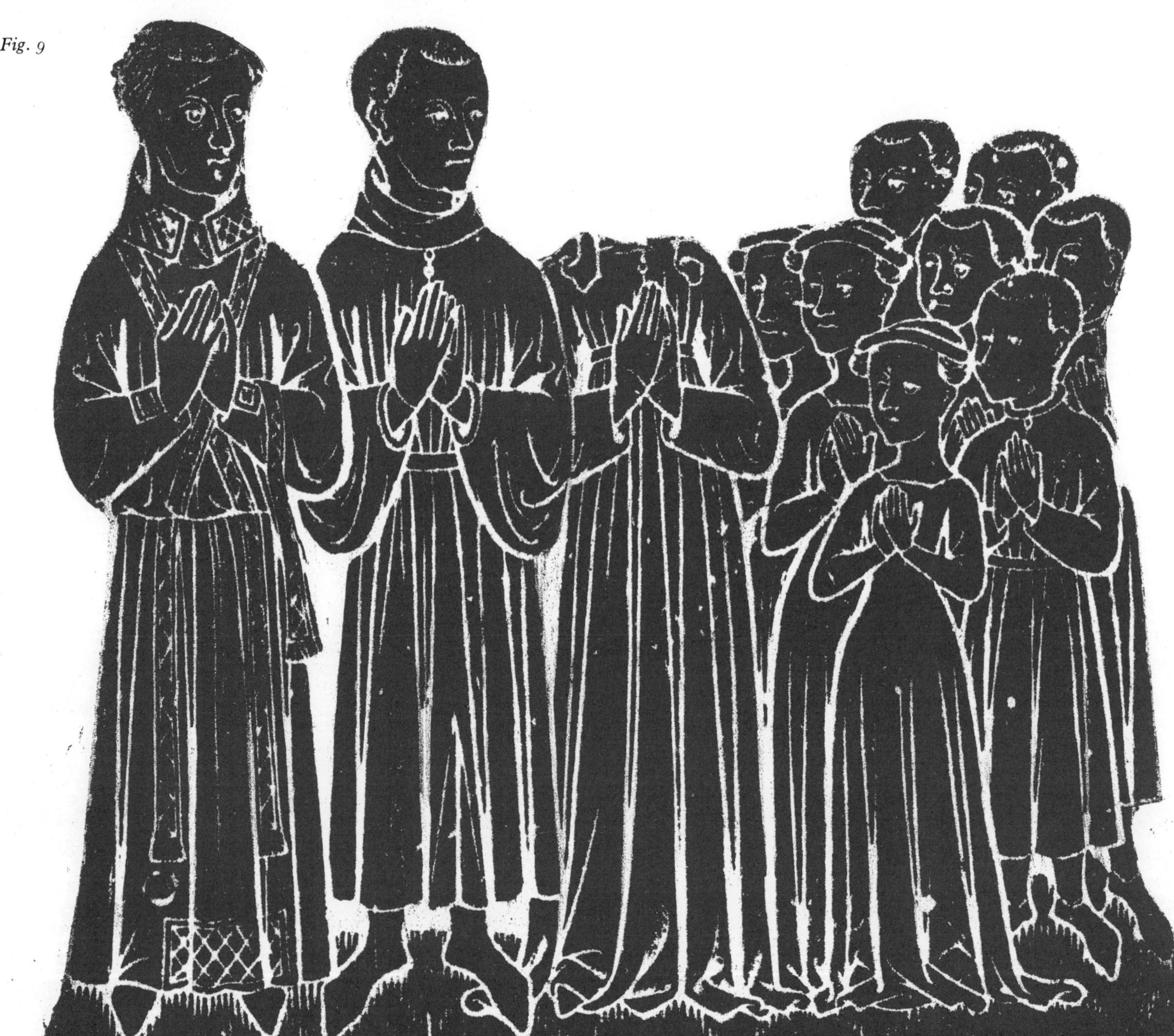

Fig. 10

This brass is 70 years later and contrasts with Fig. 9 in showing how children could be represented as separate figures, spaced out across the slab beneath the feet of their parents. For the illustration they are placed close to one another. Their father was John Lambard, citizen, mercer and alderman of London (d. 1487). William, in almuce, was rector of St Leonards, Foster Lane, London. His almuce and his sister's hat were once filled with lead or pigment. Floor of chancel, Hinxworth, Herts. Height of William 11¼ inches.

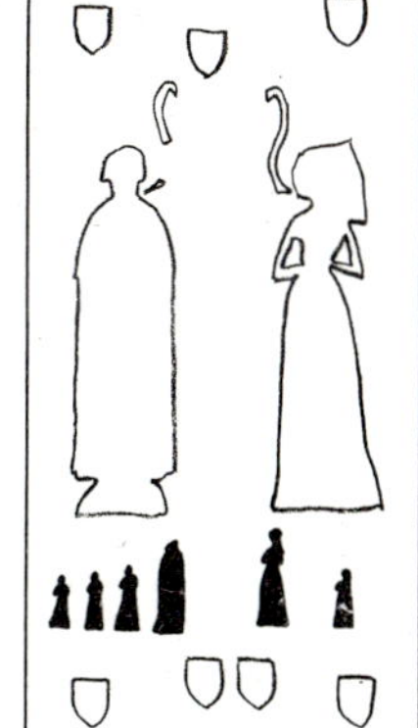

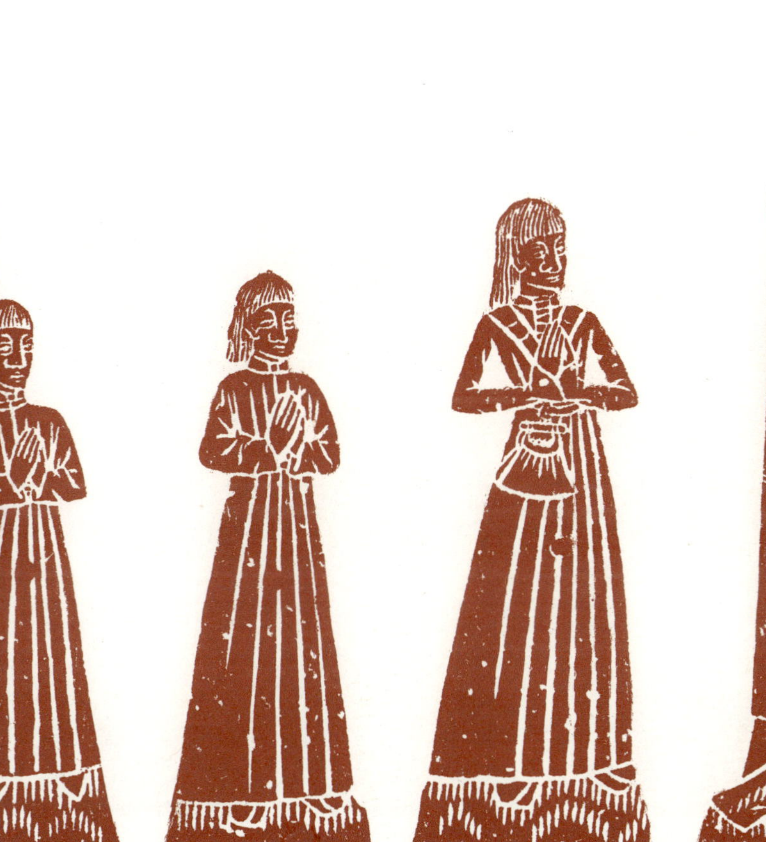

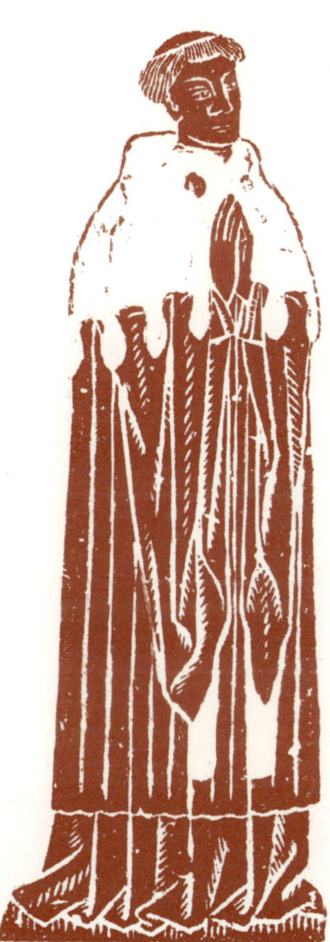

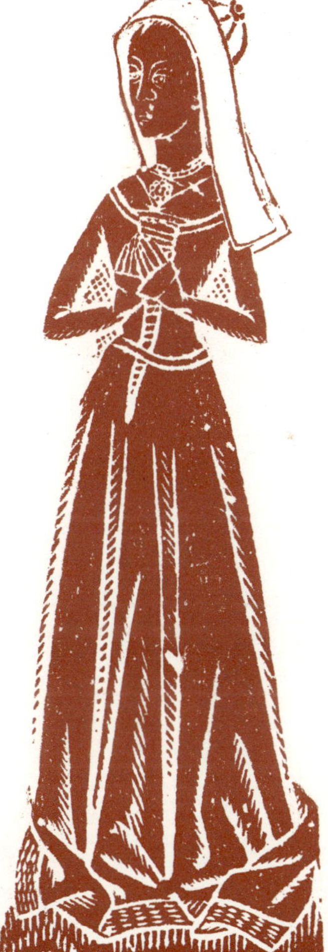

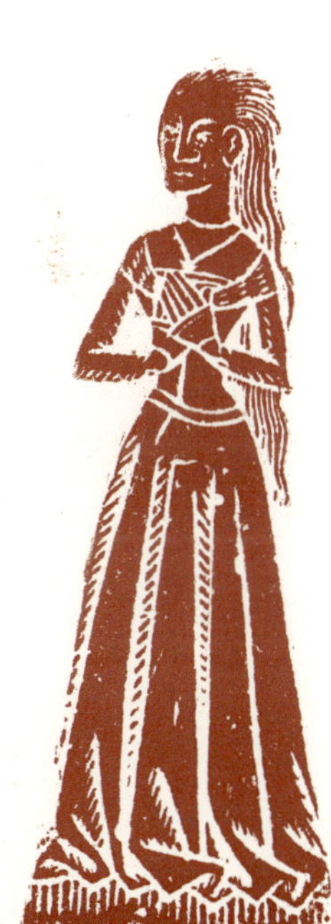

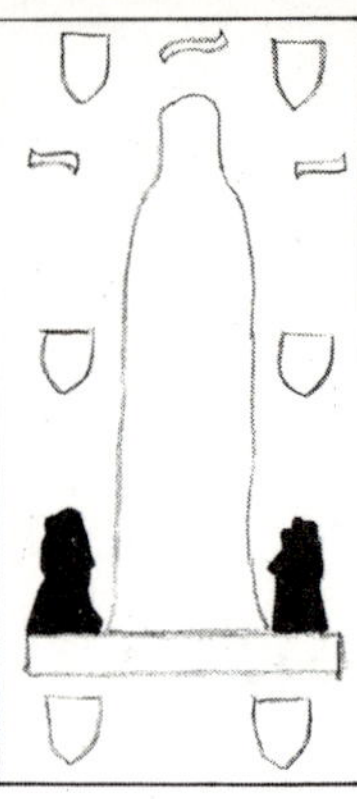

Fig. 11

The upturned faces and praying hands are perhaps derived from 'donor' pictures (see Fig. 3). These children look up towards their mother Joan (d. 1433), sometime wife of Sir Reginald Braybrook (whose pedestal sons are Fig. 5). Her last and fifth husband was Sir John Harpedon (d. 1438), whose brass is in Westminster Abbey. Chancel floor, Cobham, Kent. Height 11 inches.

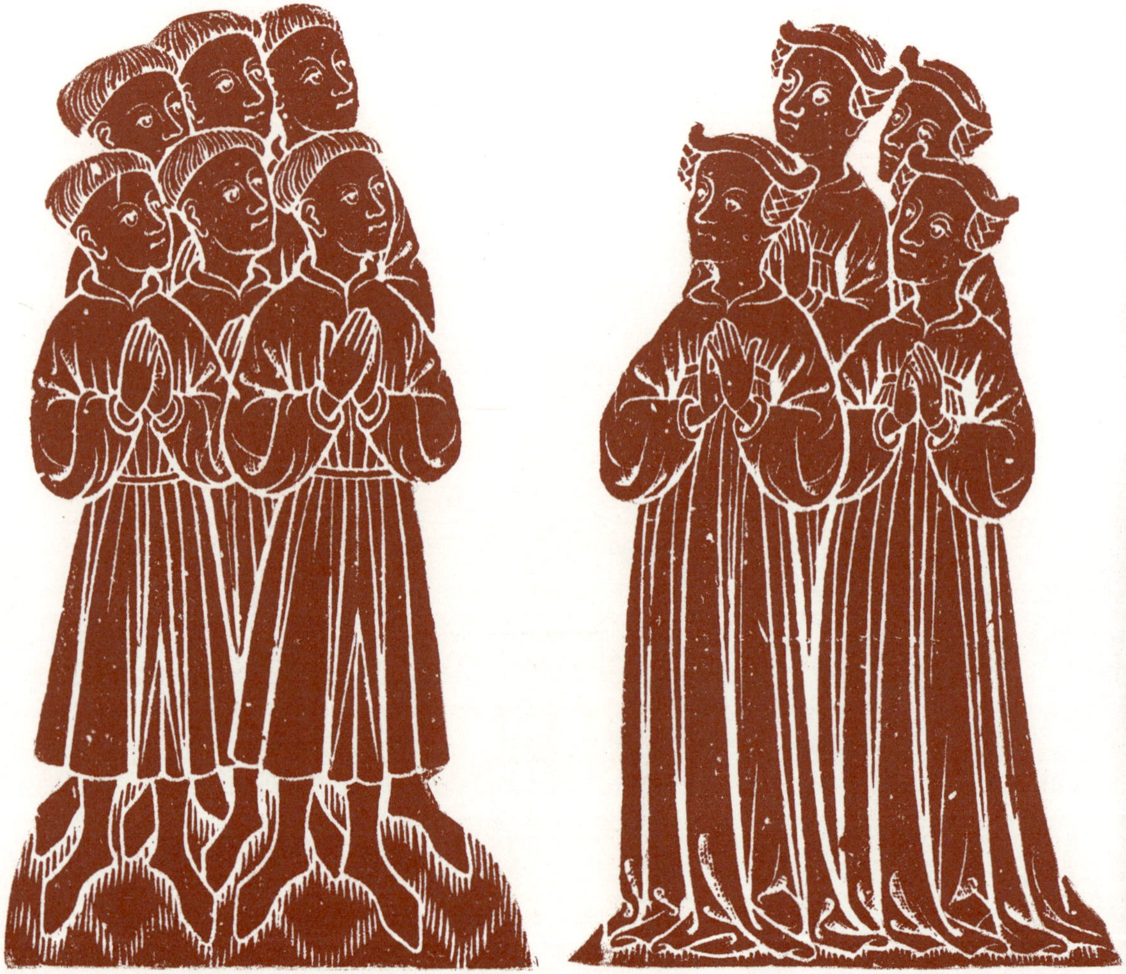

Fig. 12

This brass at Blickling, Norfolk, is a very early example of Norfolk engraving, and shows eleven sons and five daughters standing in front of their father, Roger Felthorpe (d. 1454), and their mother, Cecilie. The brass is slightly worn, on the nave floor. Height of adults only 12 inches.

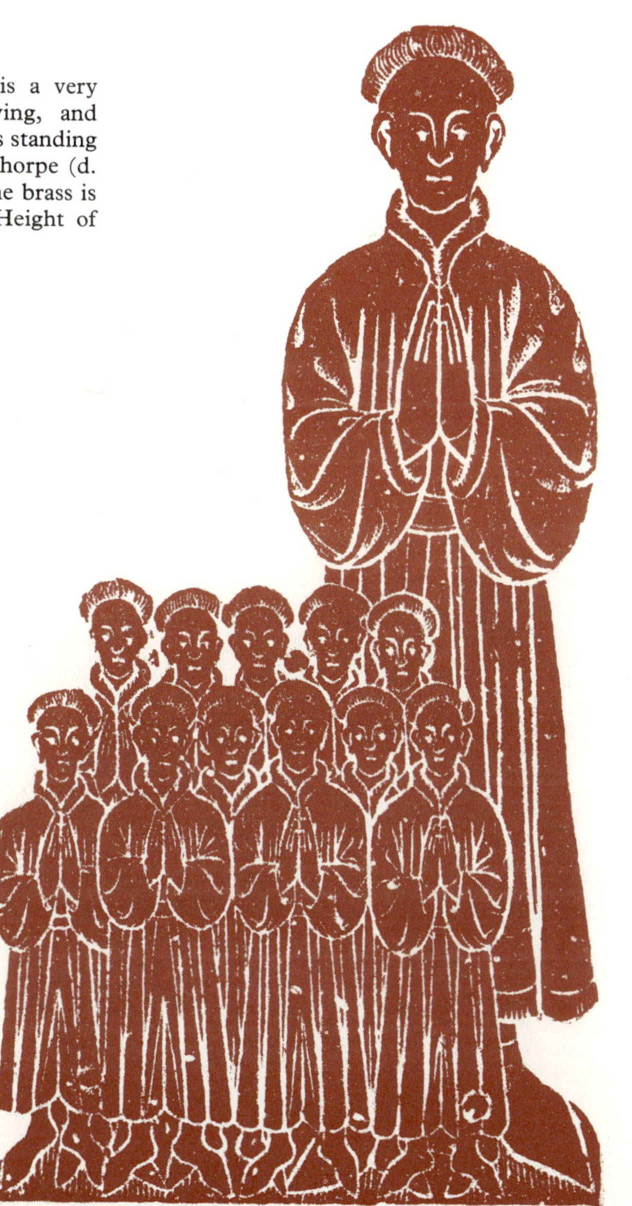

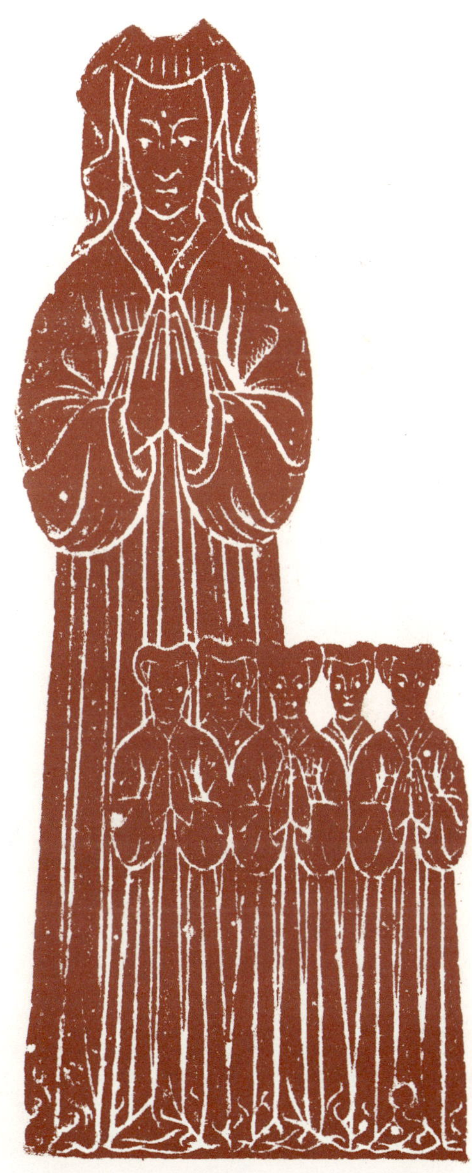

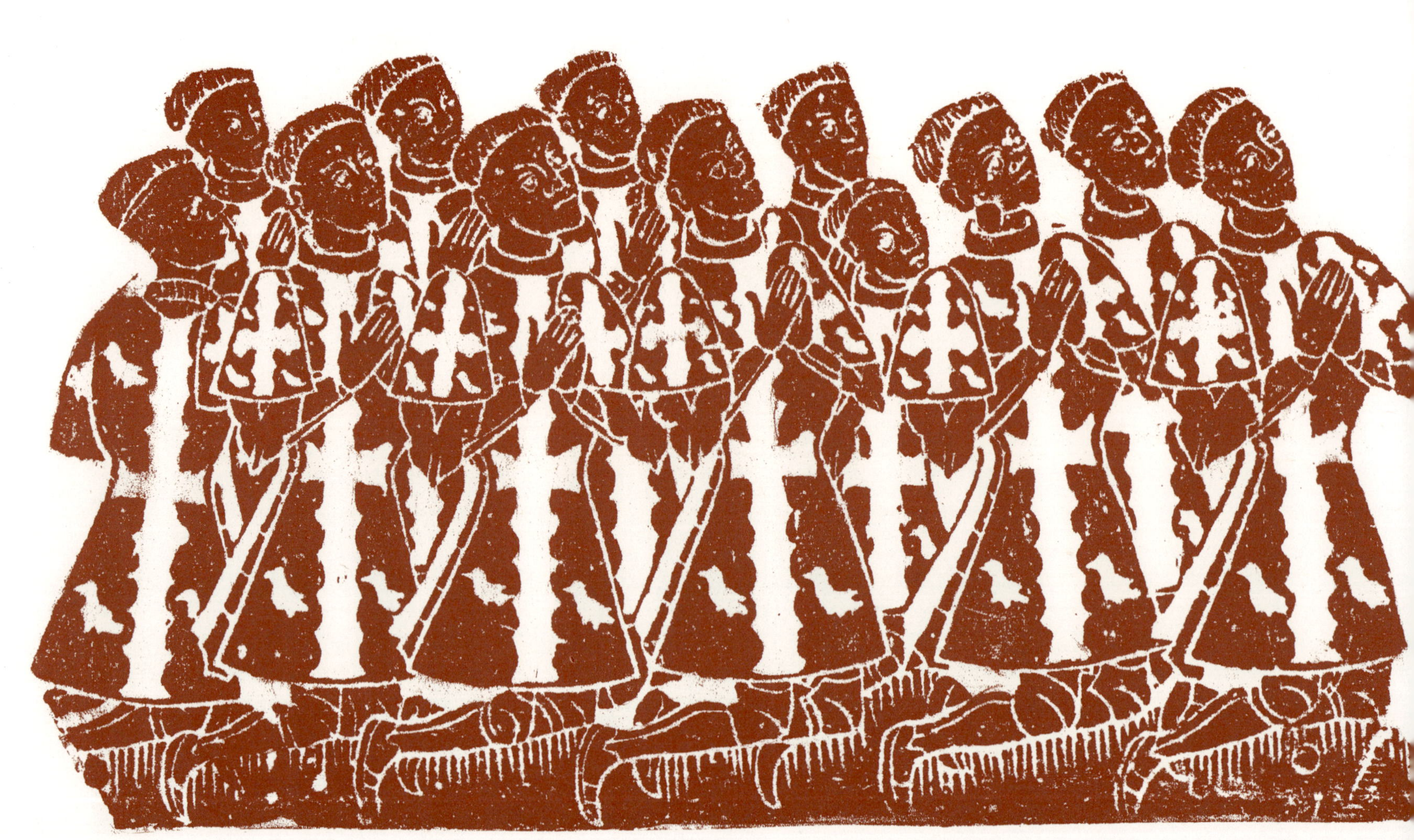

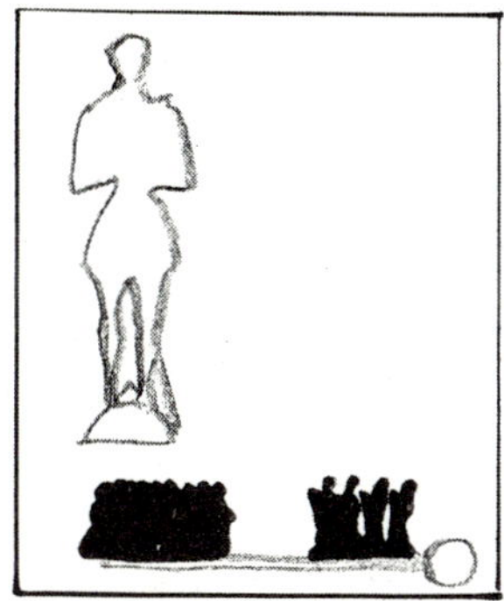

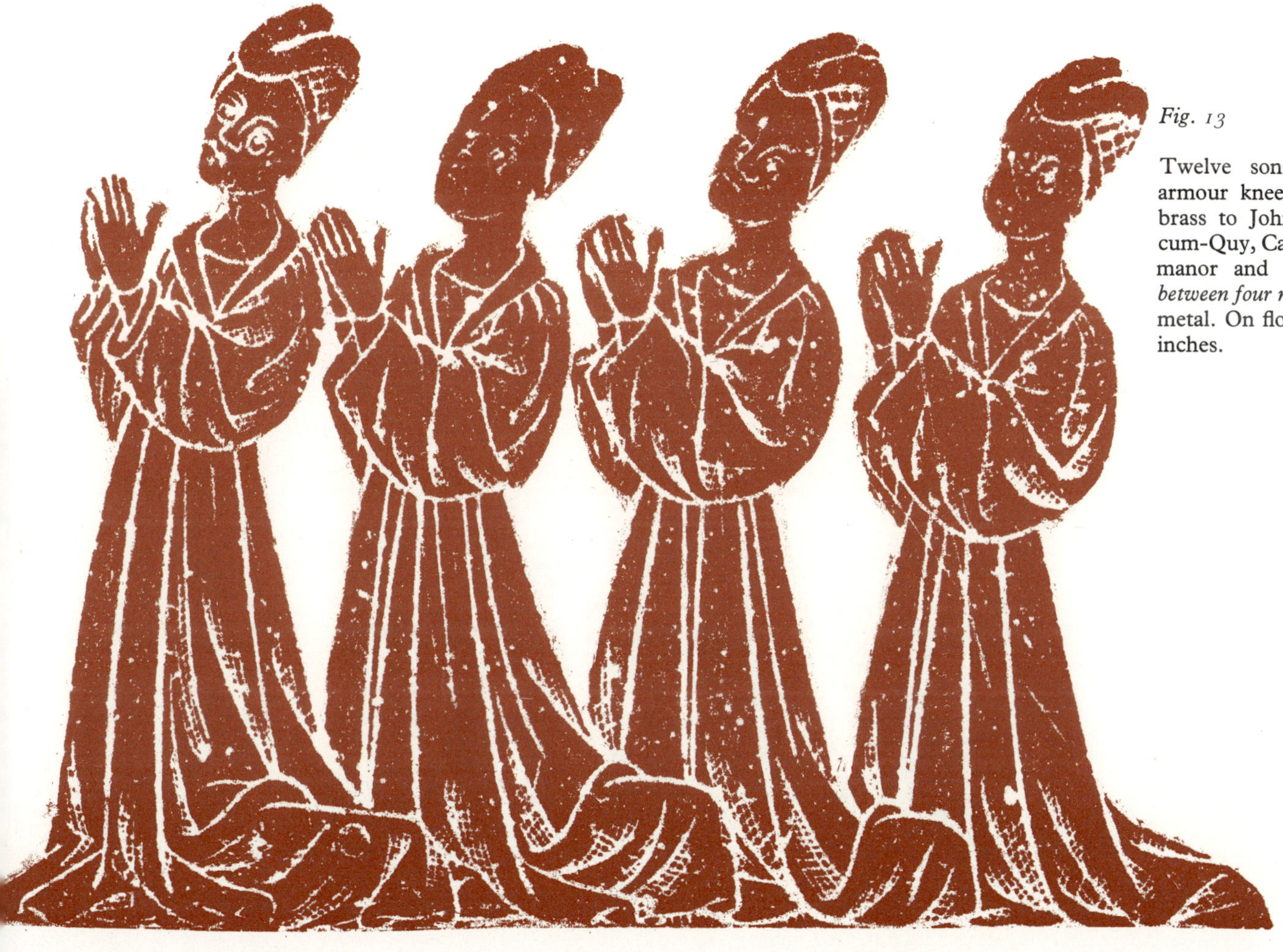

Fig. 13

Twelve sons wearing tabards over their armour kneel opposite four daughters on a brass to John Ansty and his wife in Stow-cum-Quy, Cambs. Their father was lord of the manor and his arms *or, a cross engrailed between four martlets, gu.* once added colour to metal. On floor by pulpit. Width of sons 12½ inches.

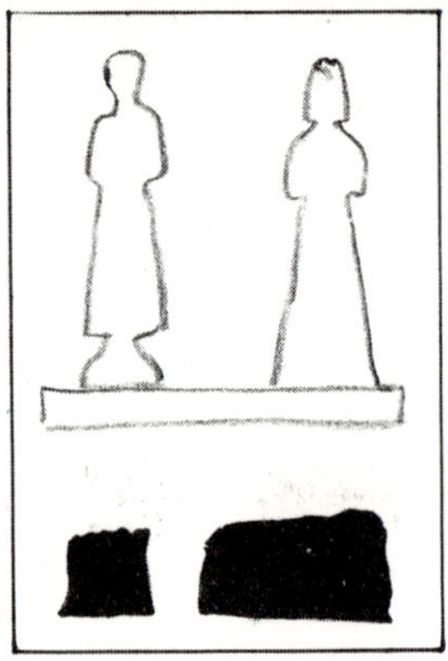

Fig. 14

There is great variety and attraction in groups of children *c.* 1450–1500. These are the children of Roger Kyngdon (d. 1471) and his wife Joan. The first son Walter wears an almuce and was parson of St Martins by Looe. The second, Edward, wears a badge on his shoulder, and was a Yeoman of the Crown. On floor of south transept, Quethioc, Cornwall. Width of sons 17 inches.

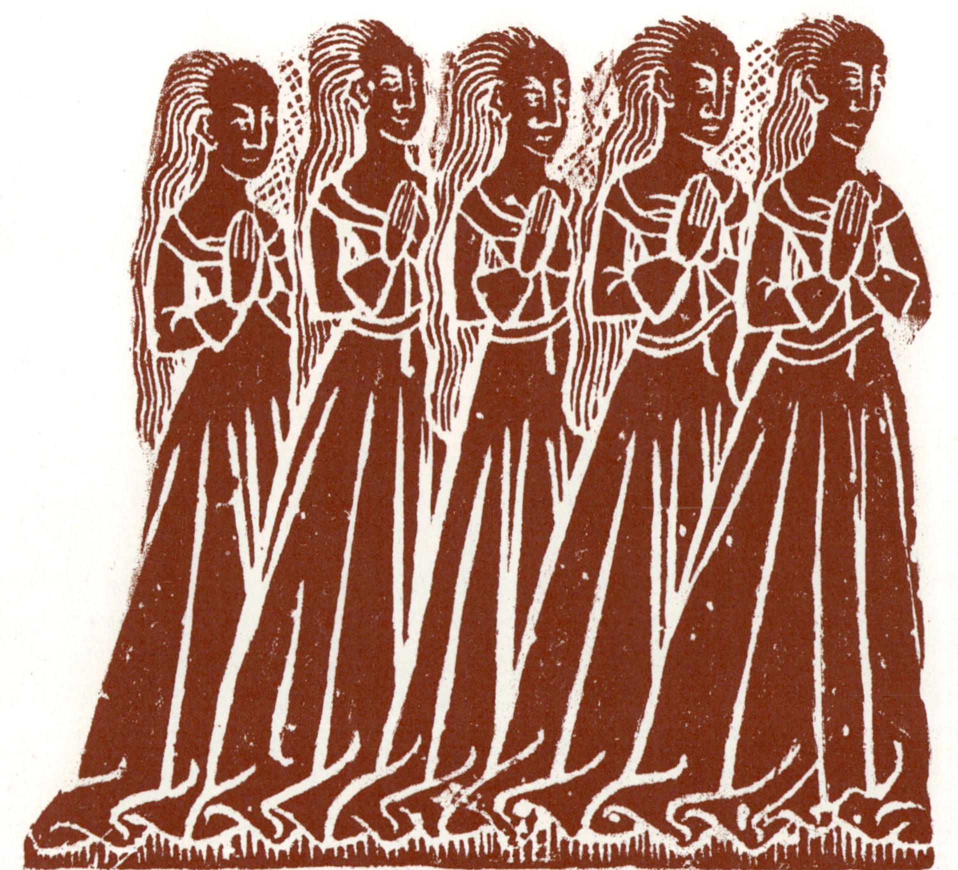

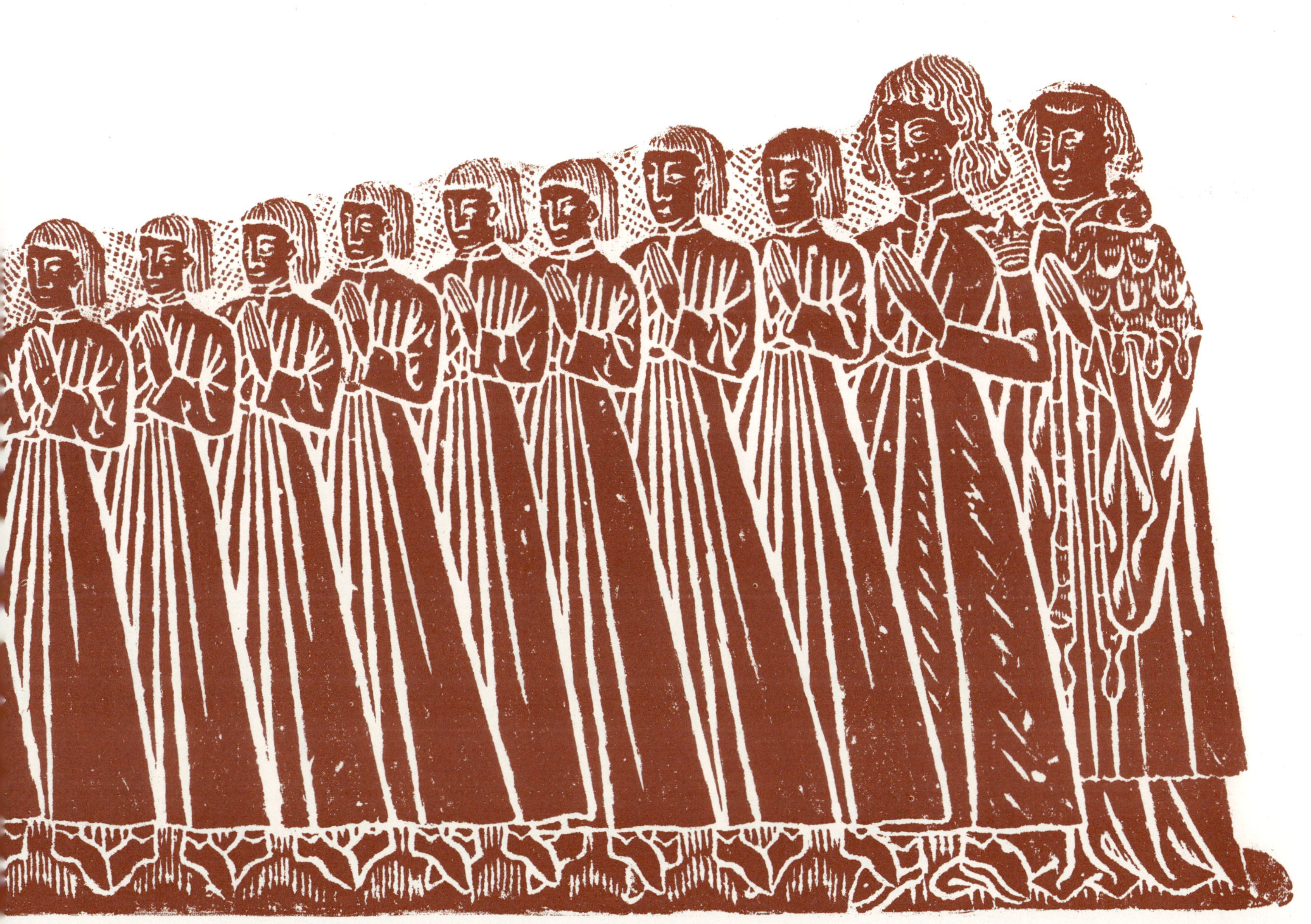

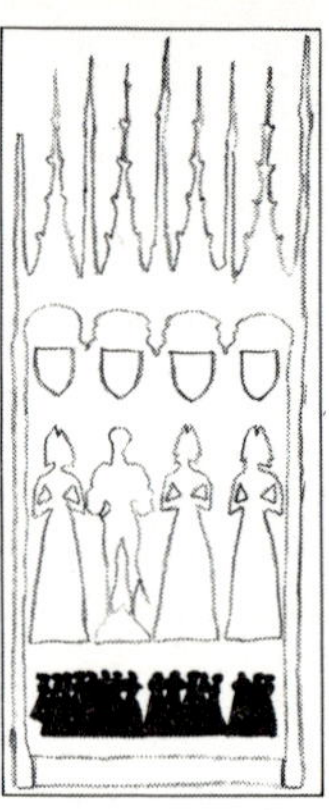

Fig. 15

Robert Ingylton was lord of the manor of Thornton, Bucks, and his magnificent brass shows him in armour beside his three wives, under a compact quadruple canopy, less than 40 inches wide. The children are arranged carefully beneath their respective mothers. On altar tomb, Thornton. Width of children 29 inches.

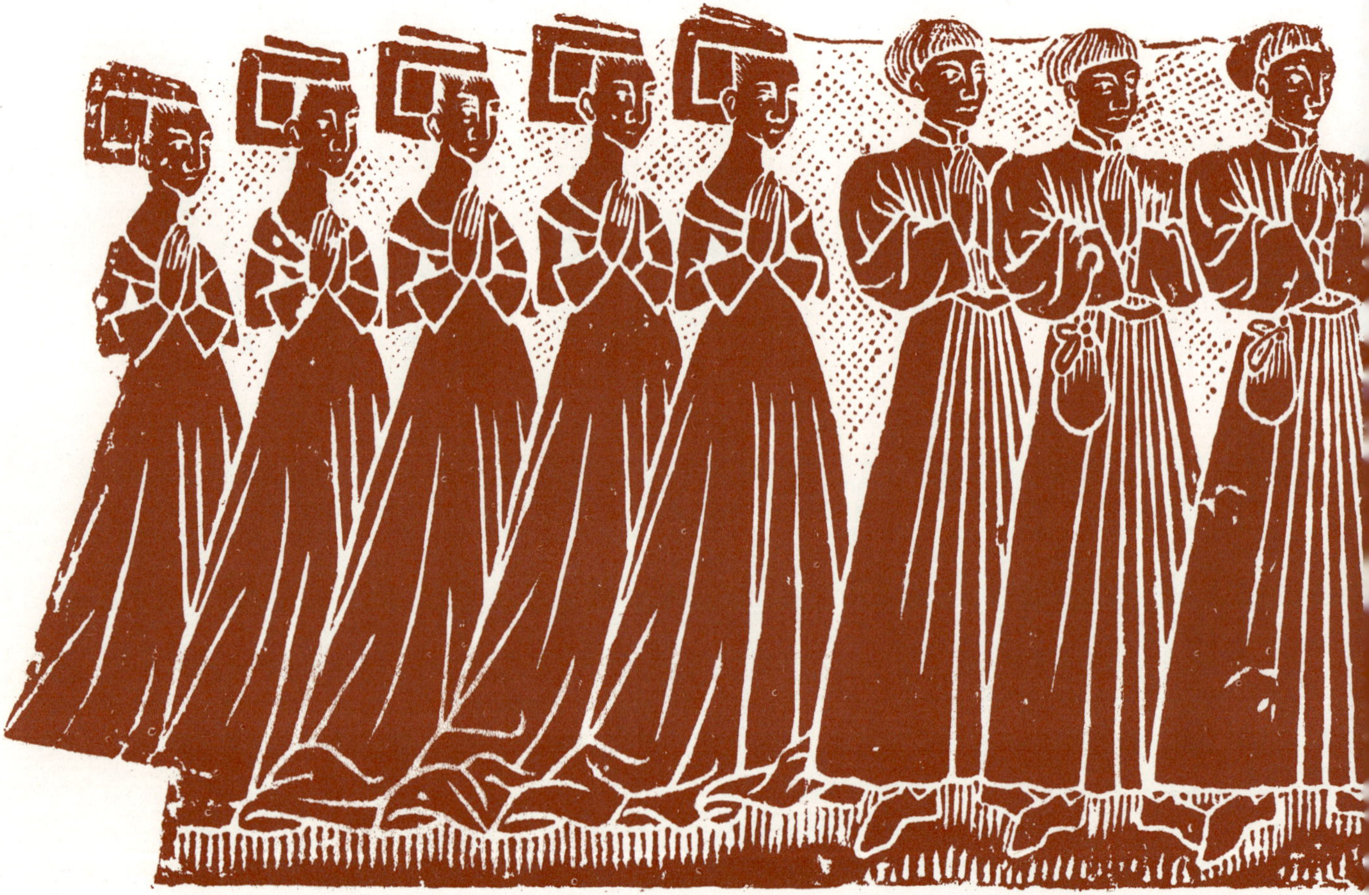

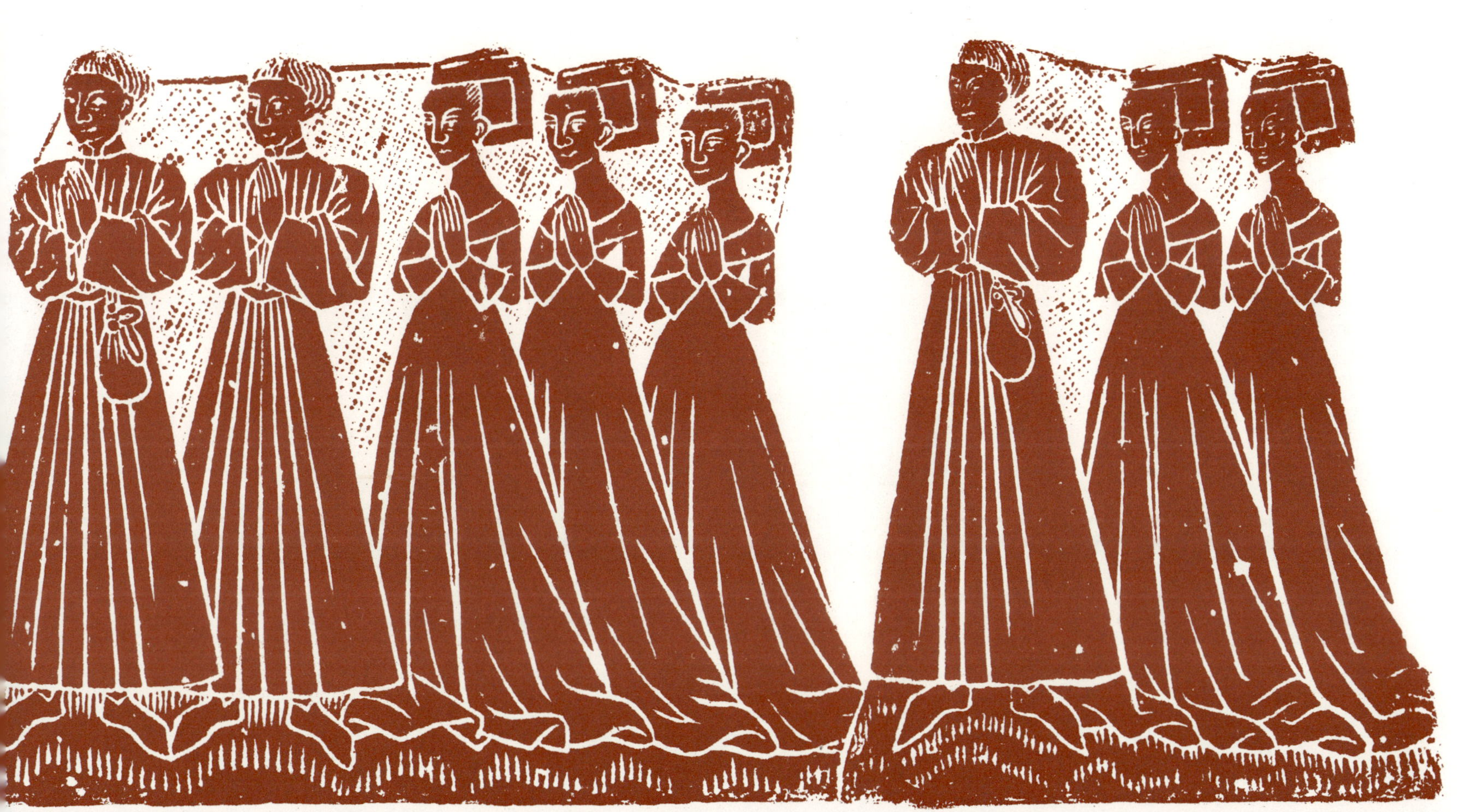

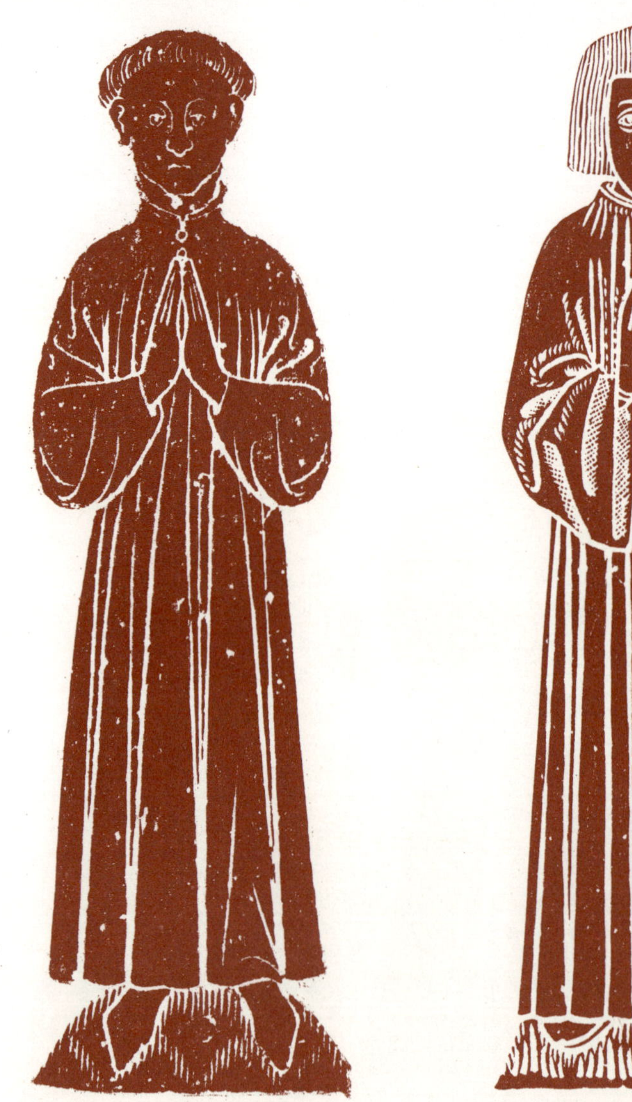

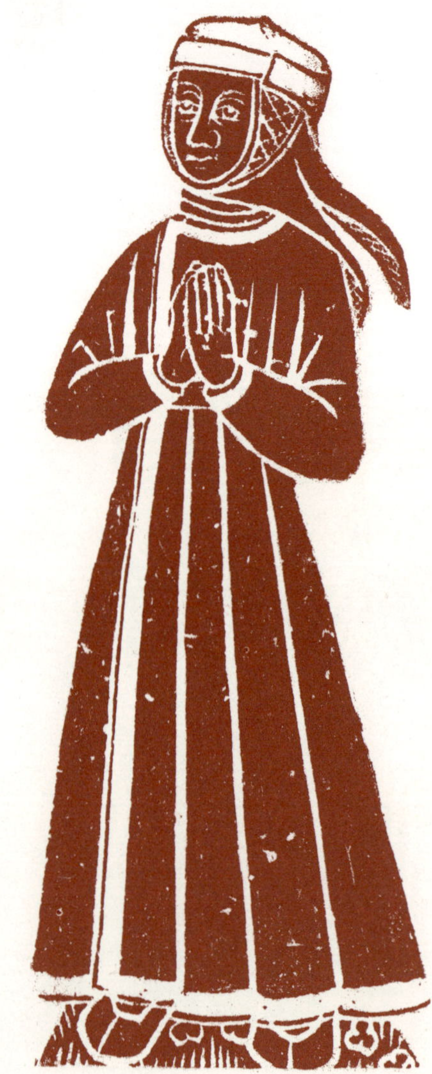

Figs. 16, 17, 18

The boy on the left is John Kent, a Winchester scholar (d. 1434), height 12¼ inches. On the right, John Stonor (d. 1512) may be an Eton scholar. Height 12 inches. Thomas Heron in the centre, height 16½ inches died aged fourteen in 1517; his father Sir John Heron was the King's private treasurer. Note the pencase and ink pot hanging from his waist; these and John Stonor's hat and gown trimming are deeply recessed to carry pigment.

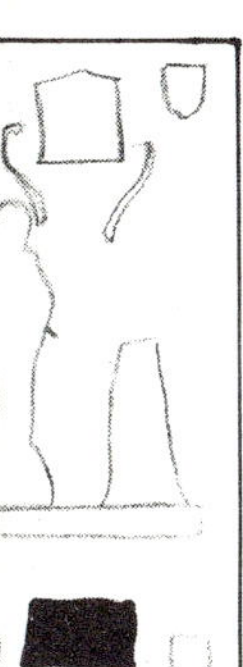

Fig. 19

The two sons and six daughters of Thomas (d. 1483) and Isabel Hampton. The daughters are arranged two by two, the younger with berets and loose hair, the elder with butterfly head-dresses (veils omitted), and the eldest with slight cleavage. On altar tomb in chancel Stoke Charity, Hampshire. Width 12½ inches.

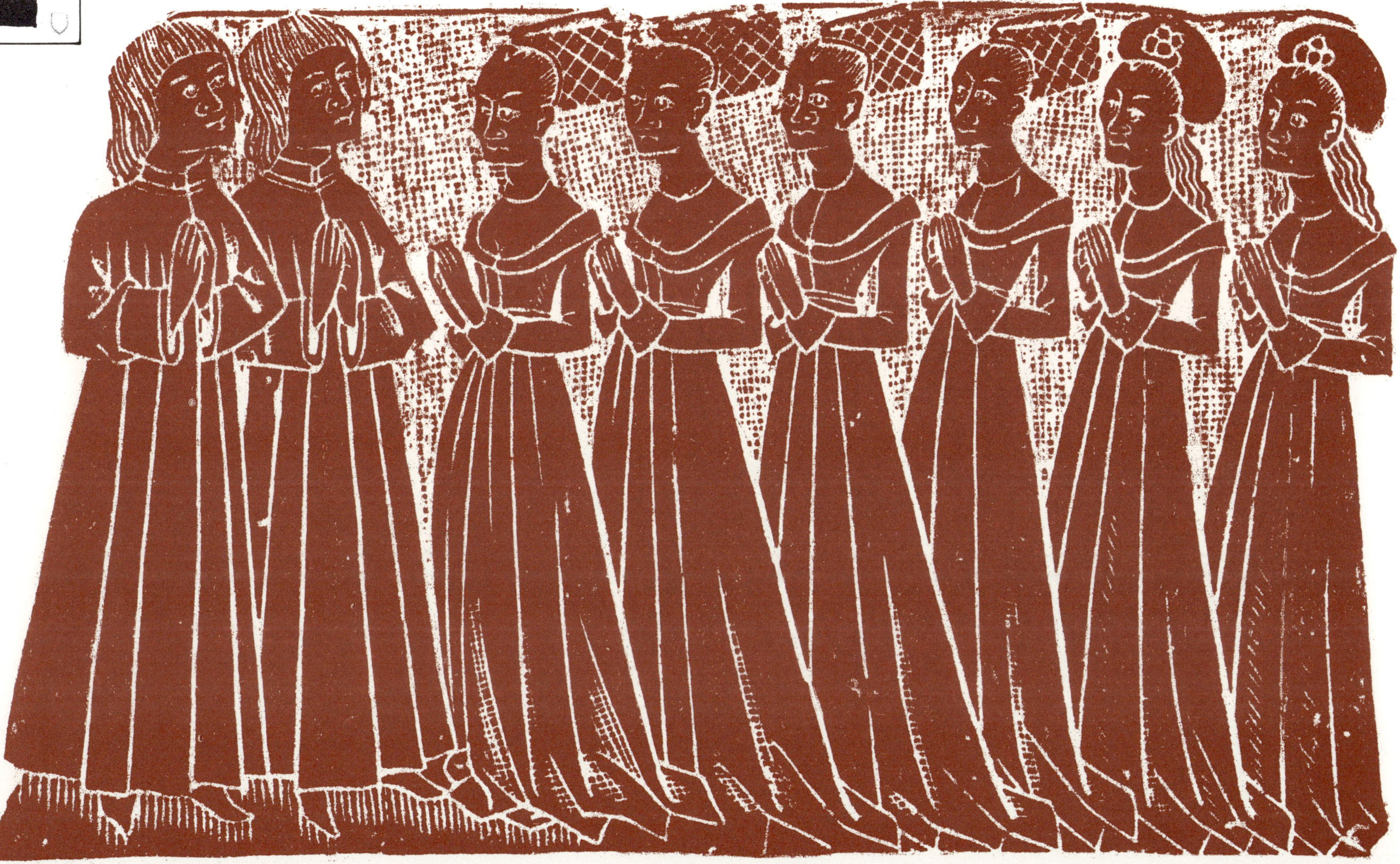

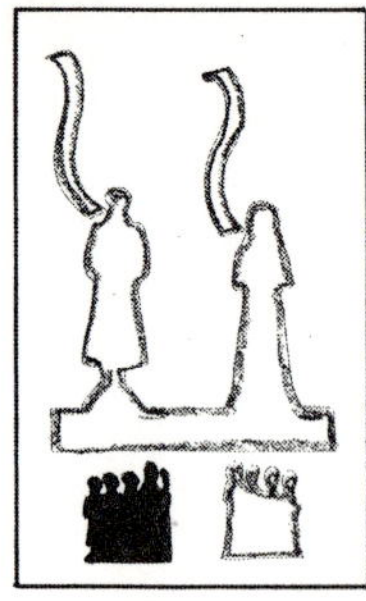

Fig. 20

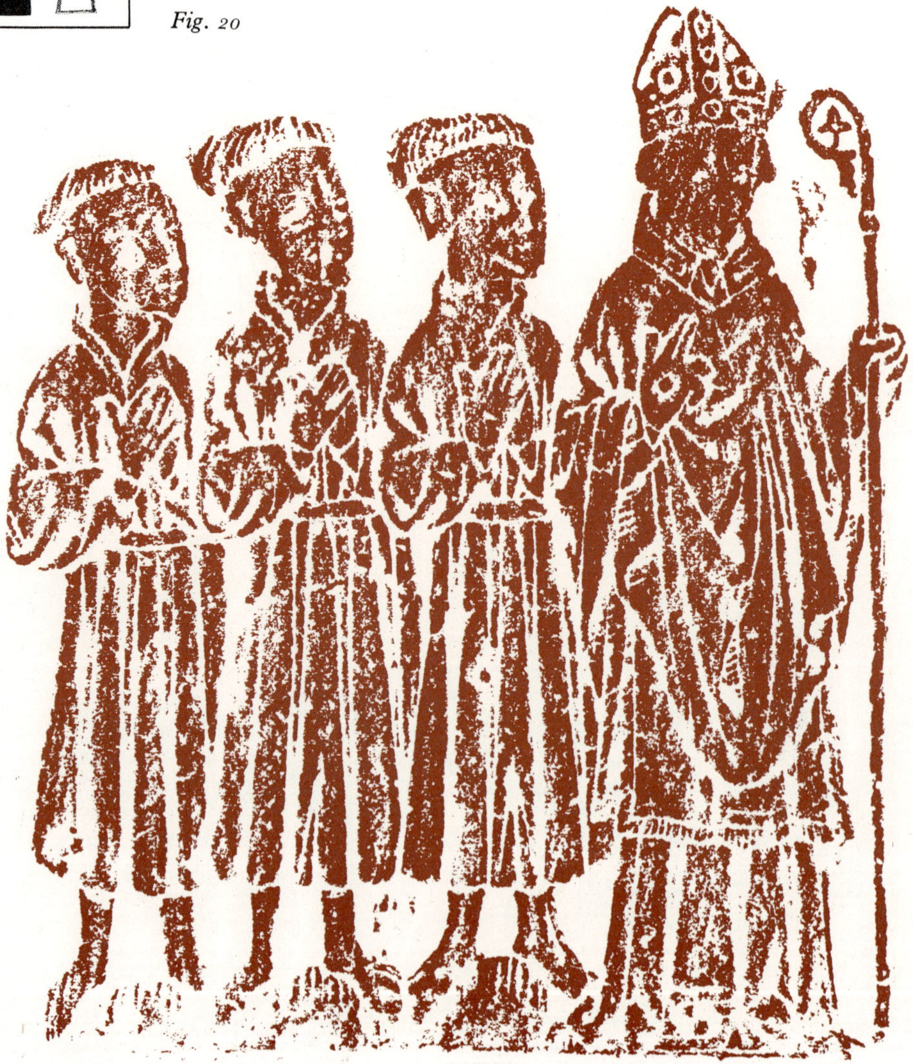

Fig. 20

These sons of William Lucas and his wife Katherine, *c.* 1460, were stolen during the 1939–45 war from Wendon Lofts, Essex. The eldest son, John, became Abbot of Waltham. Illustrated from an old rubbing in the Society of Antiquaries, London. Same scale. The slab and remaining parts of metal now in Elmdon, Essex.

Fig. 21, right

The four sons of Robert and Elizabeth Warham, who lived at Malshanger house. The eldest, William, in academic attire, became Archbishop of Canterbury and travelled abroad on various political missions. He crowned Henry VIII and Catherine of Aragon and later became involved in dissolving their marriage. On altar tomb, south aisle, Oakley, Hants. Same scale.

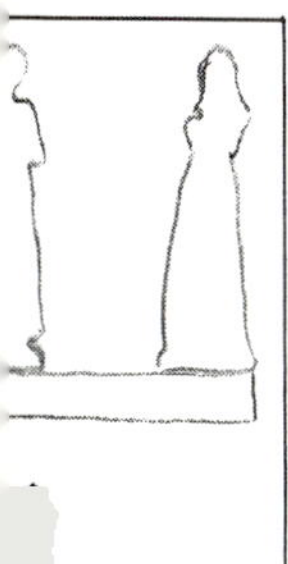

Fig. 21

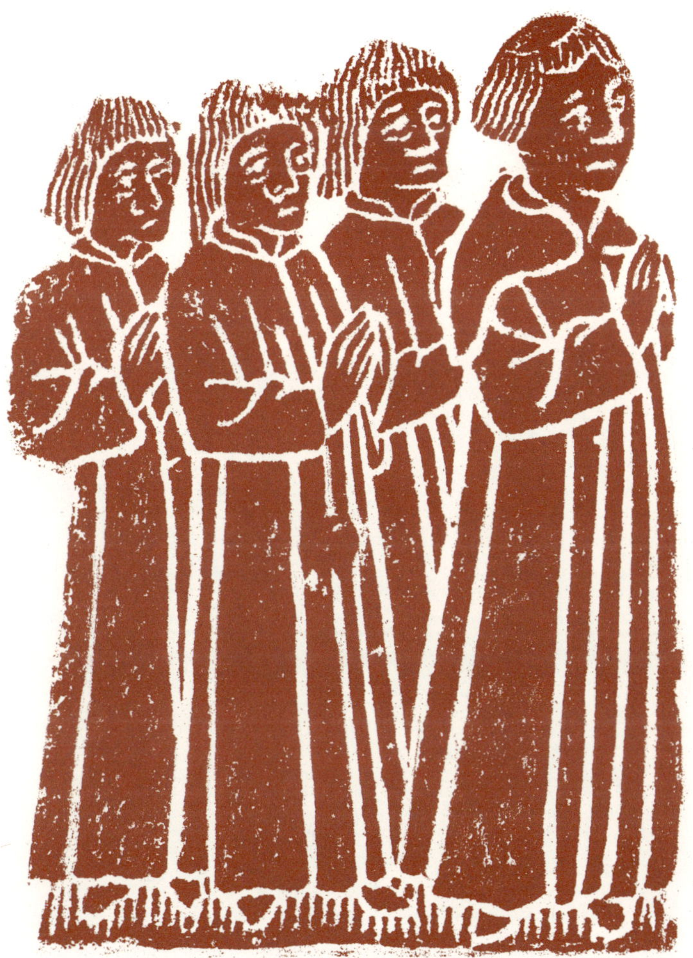

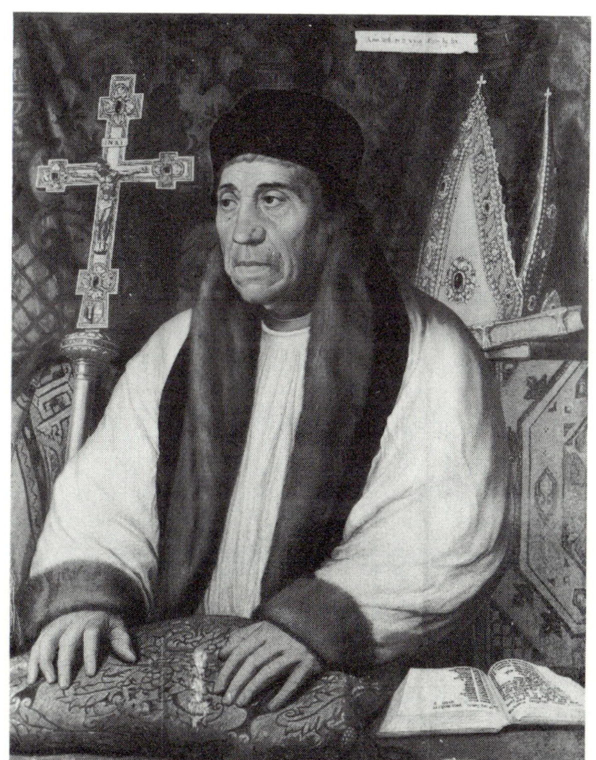

Fig. 22

A portrait of Archbishop William Warham, attributed to Holbein. National Portrait Gallery, London. Width 26 inches.

Fig. 23

As in Fig. 15, these are the segregated children of three mothers, the wives of George Ainsworth (d. 1488). One son, slightly taller than the rest, is dressed as a priest. On wall of south transept, Harrow, Middlesex. Same scale.

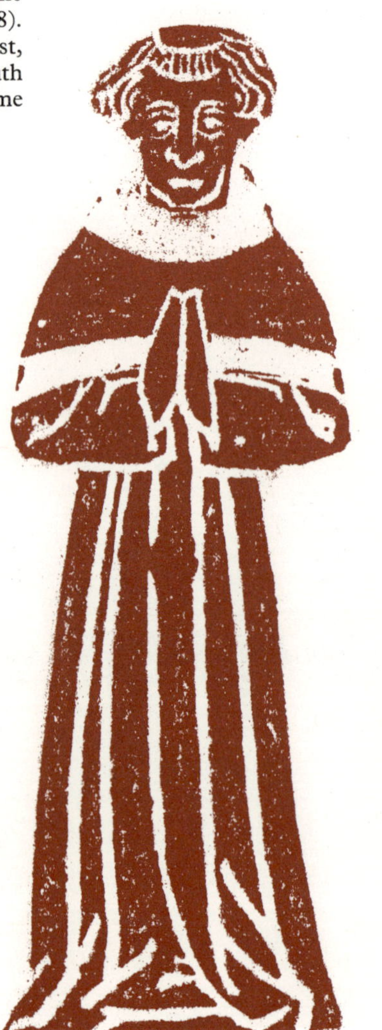

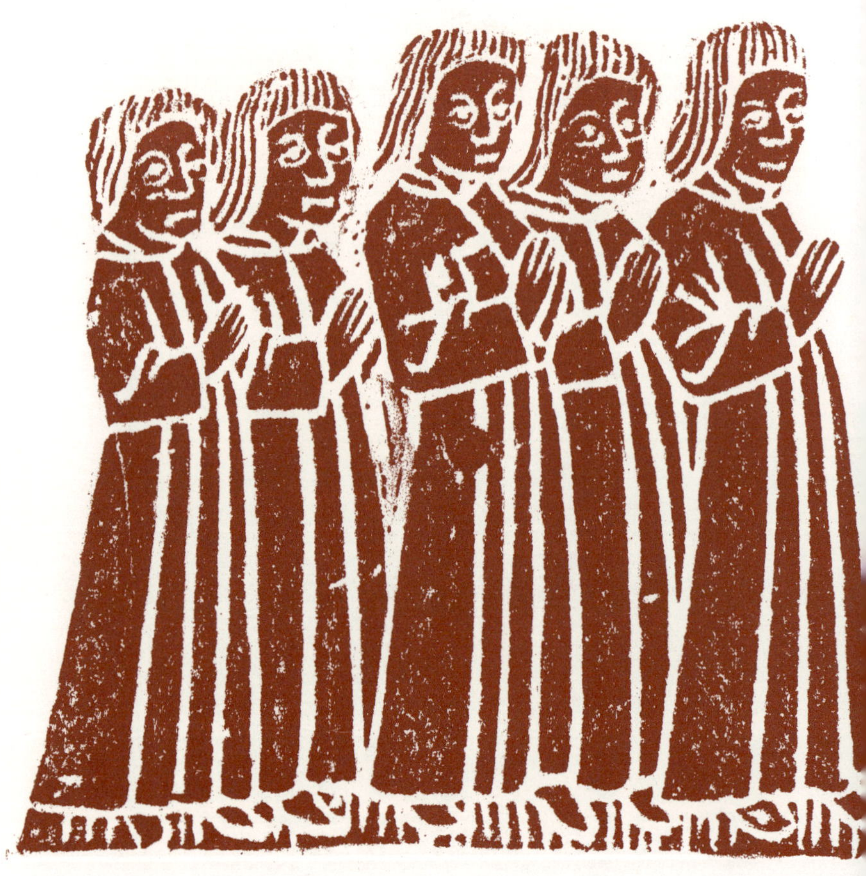

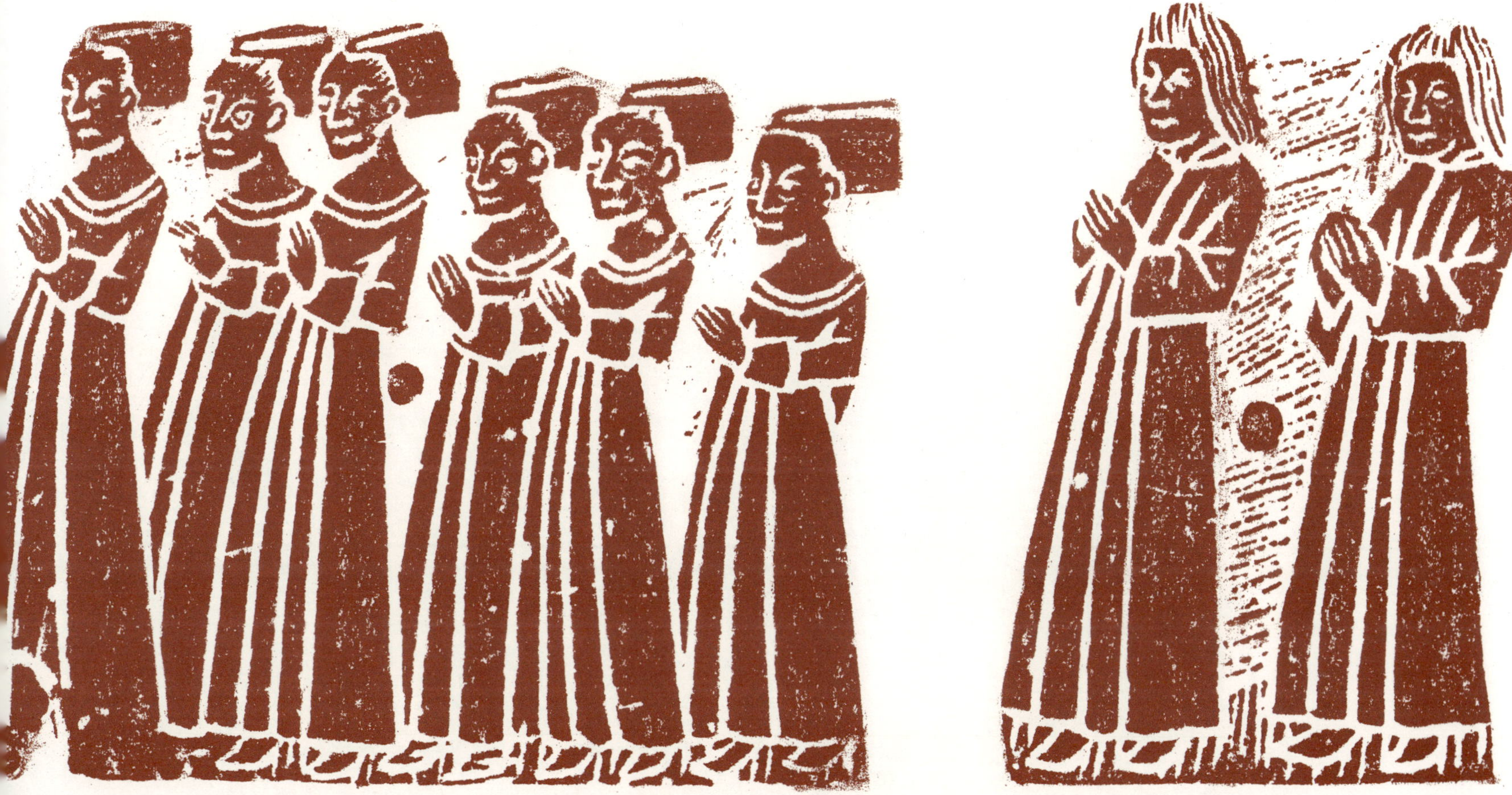

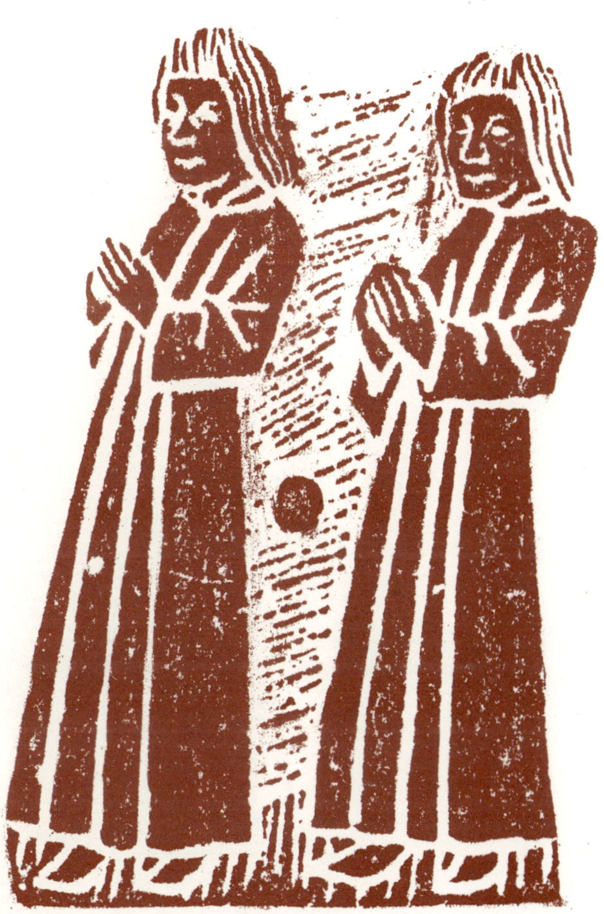

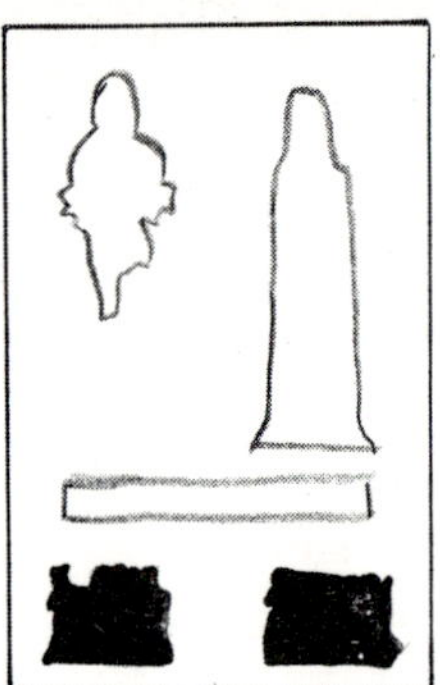

Fig. 24

The children of Thomas Mountford (d. 1489) and his wife Agnes. Such attention has been paid to the design of their children that they can be fairly closely identified by reference to the 1563–4 Visitation (Harleian Soc., Vol. XVI, p. 214). They are, in order: Henry '*Clericus*' John and John '*gemelles obierunt*' William, Christopher, and George, Thomas the eldest and (Edmund?) who '*obiit puer*'. Of the daughters, Margaret, Jane, Elenor, Anne, Margaret and Elizabeth are listed with husbands. Cecyli is not given a husband and should, therefore, be the nun. On floor at east end of south aisle, Hornby, North Riding, Yorkshire. Width of sons 10 inches.

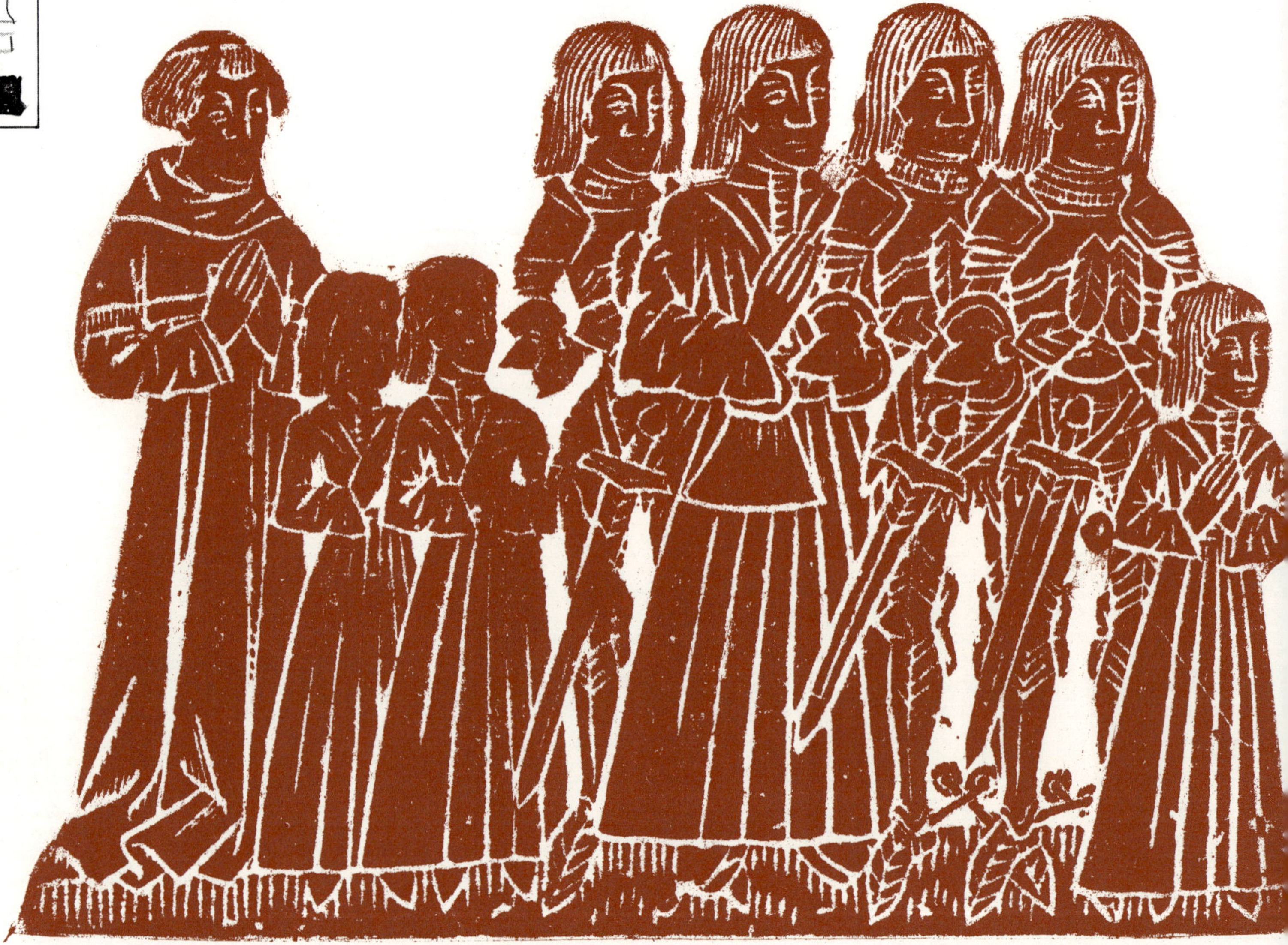

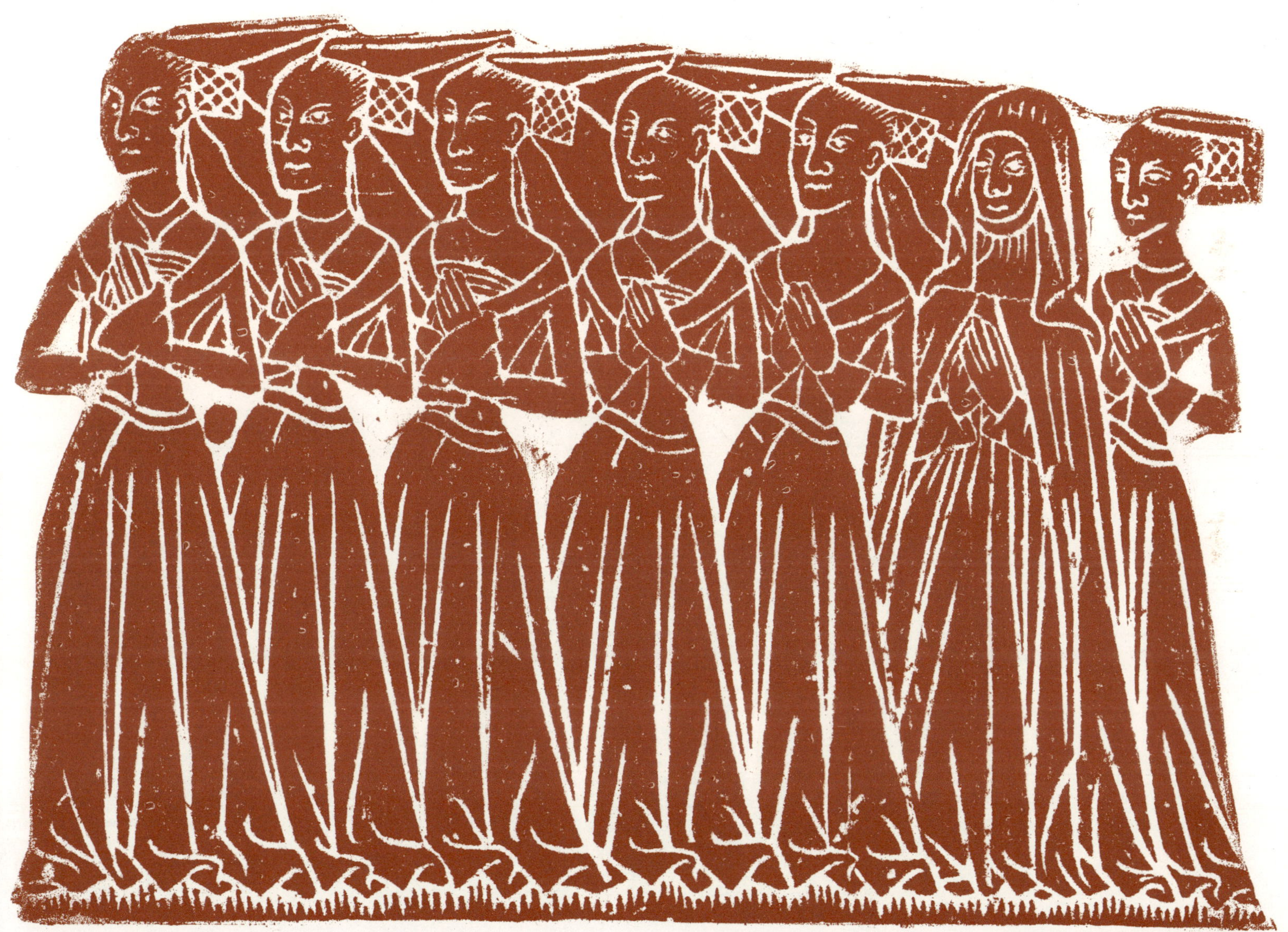

Fig. 25

One way of showing that four daughters were dead when the brass to their parents was engraved was to dress them in shrouds or winding sheets. They seem to wear the tied ends like hats. From the brass to Richard and Johane Yate (d. 1500). On wall of chancel, Longworth, Berks. Same scale.

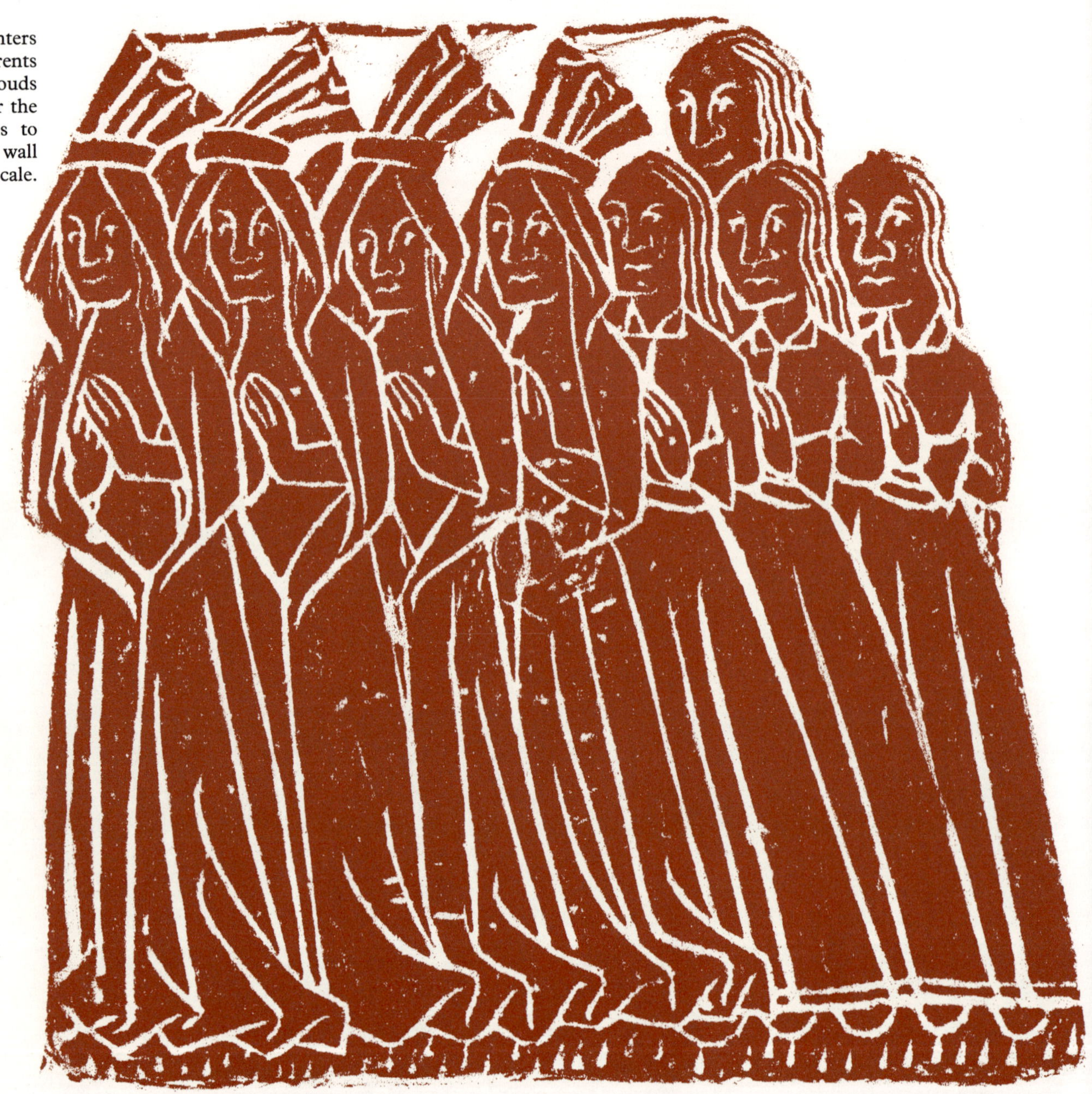

Fig. 26

Five kneeling daughters of James Pekham (d. 1500), on the floor of the nave in Wrotham, Kent. Same scale.

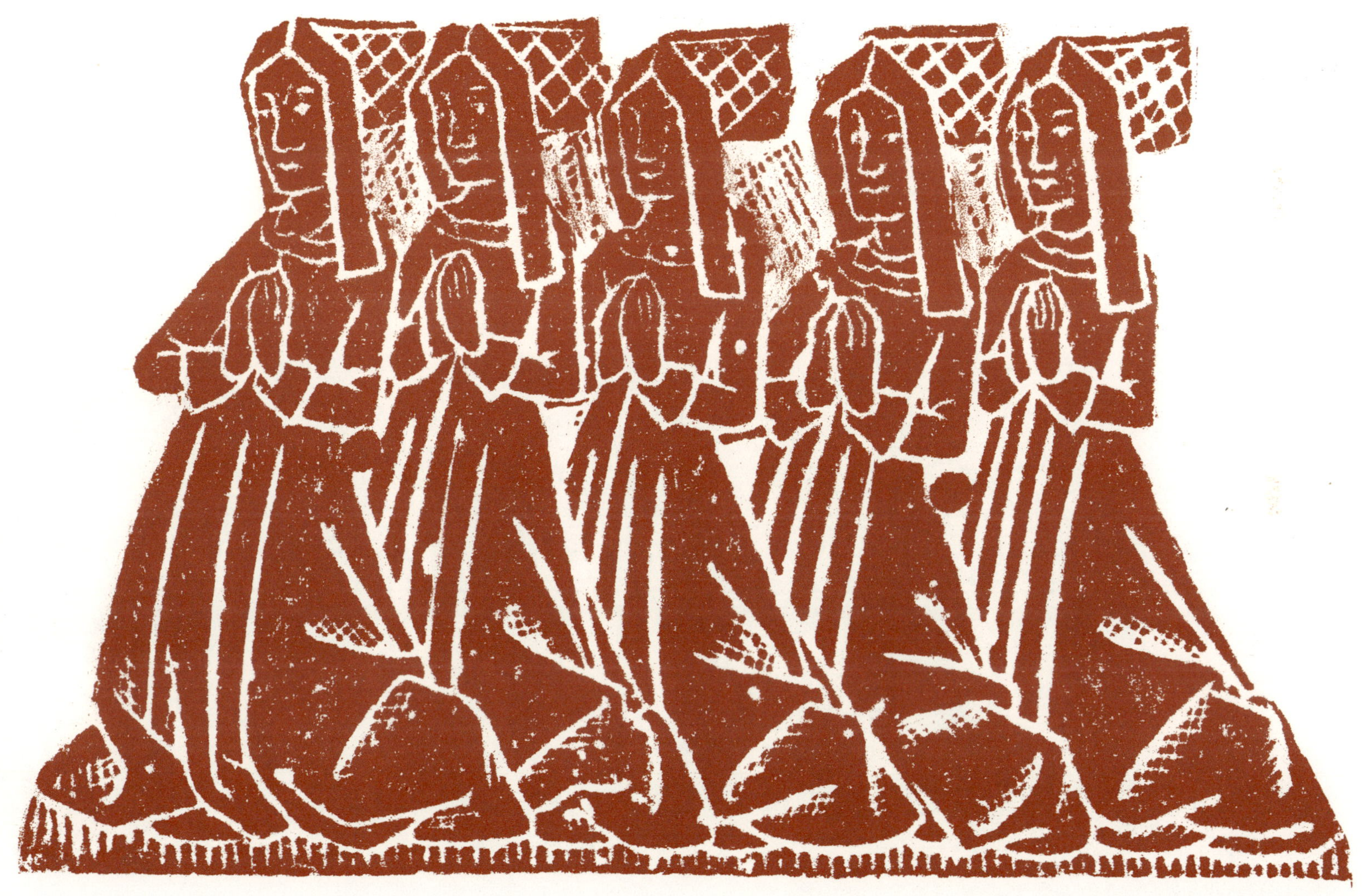

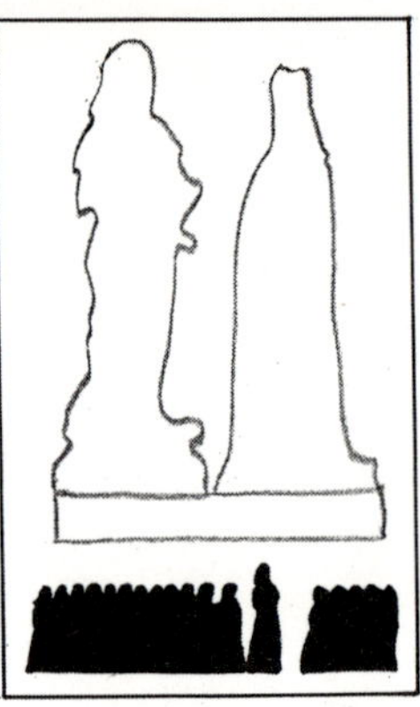

Fig. 27

A large group of thirteen sons, the eldest a separate and taller figure with a purse and the second a priest with a rosary. The daughters wear dog-kennel hats with their hair streaming down behind. Their father, as the Latin inscription tells, was Robert Baynard (d. 1501), skilled in the law and an active soldier. Their mother Elizabeth was a most loving wife, 'and had as many sons and daughters as are shown below'. The youngest son is on a separate piece of metal, suggesting that he had to be added to make the inscription accurate. Floor of south transept, Lacock, Wiltshire. Width of sons 20½ inches.

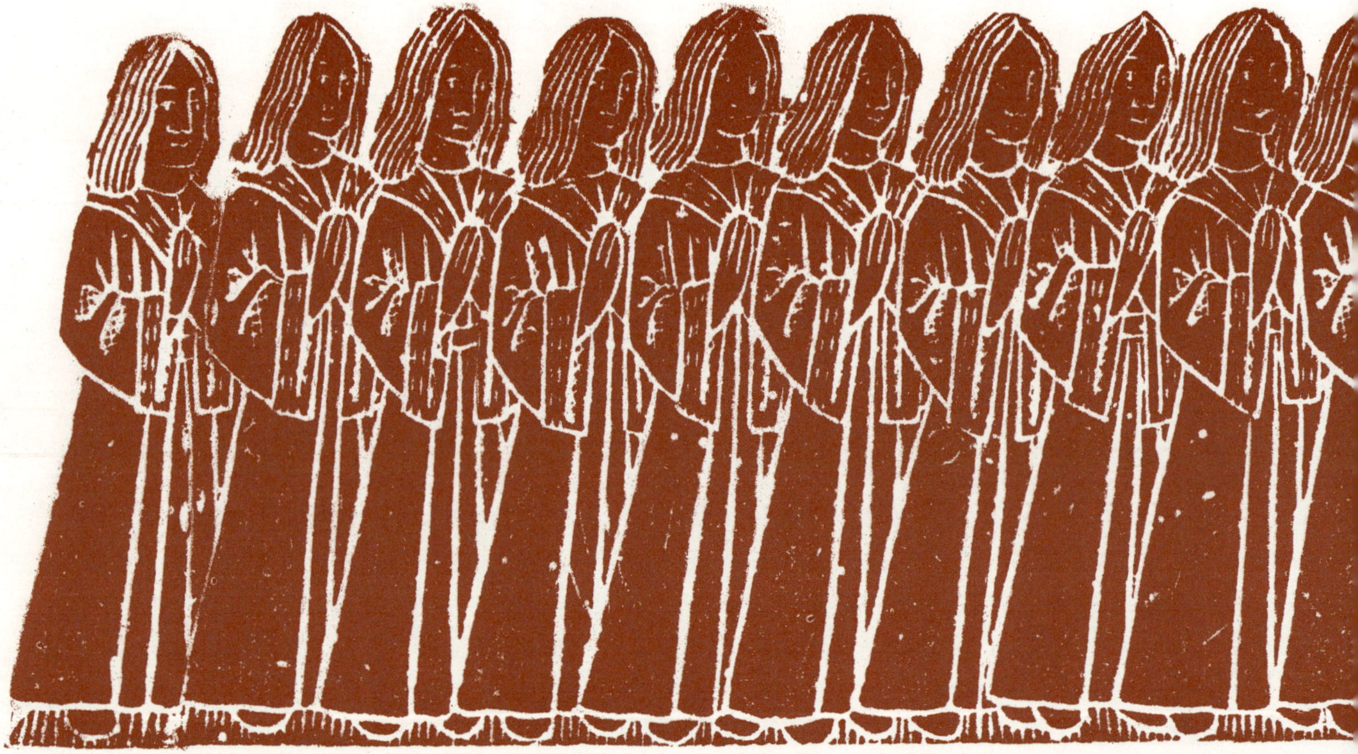

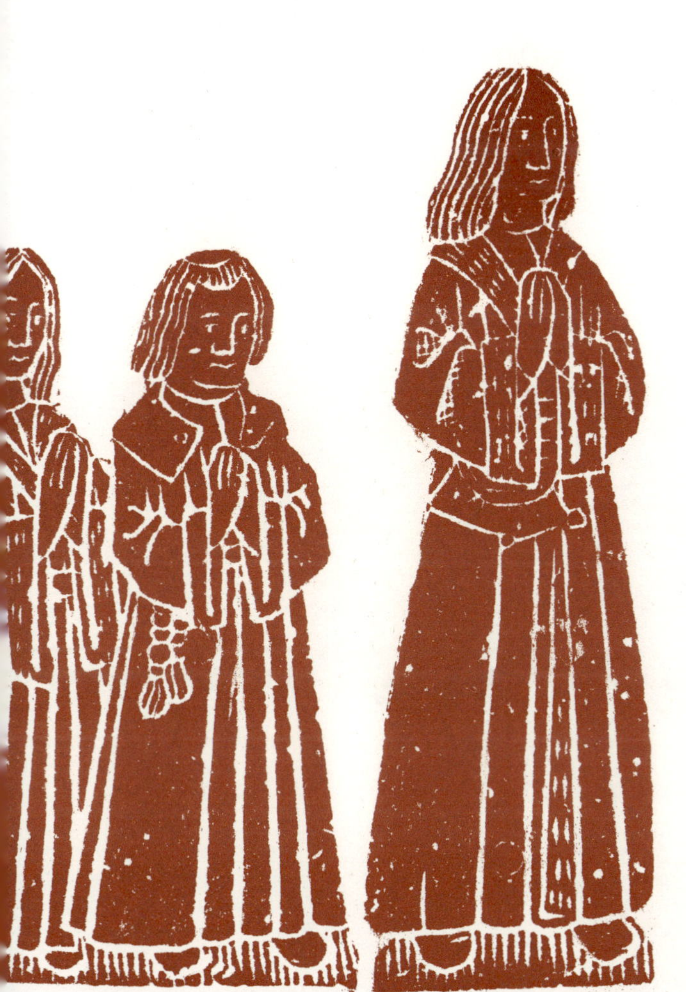

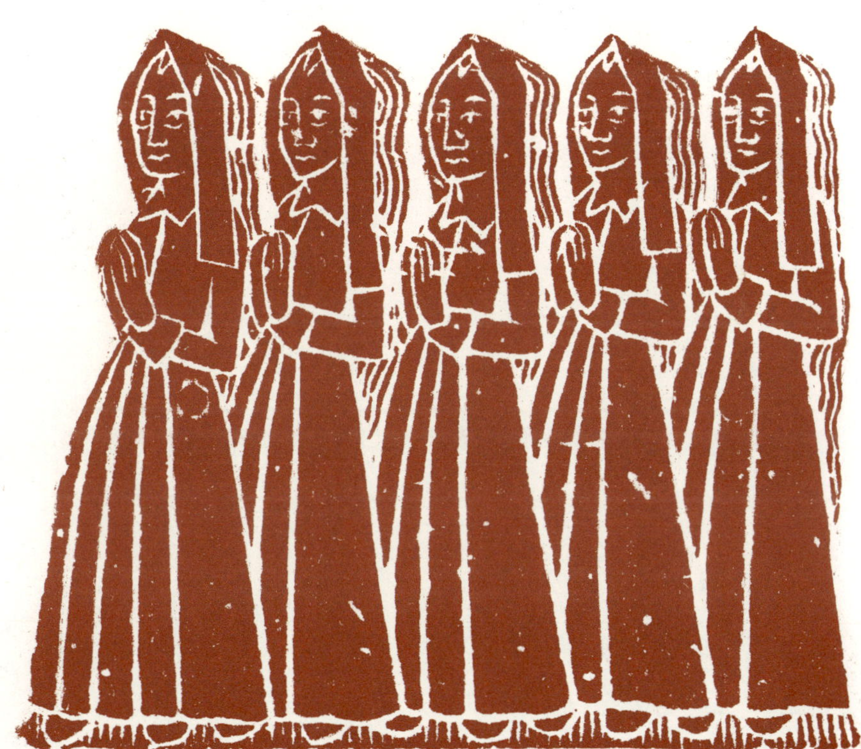

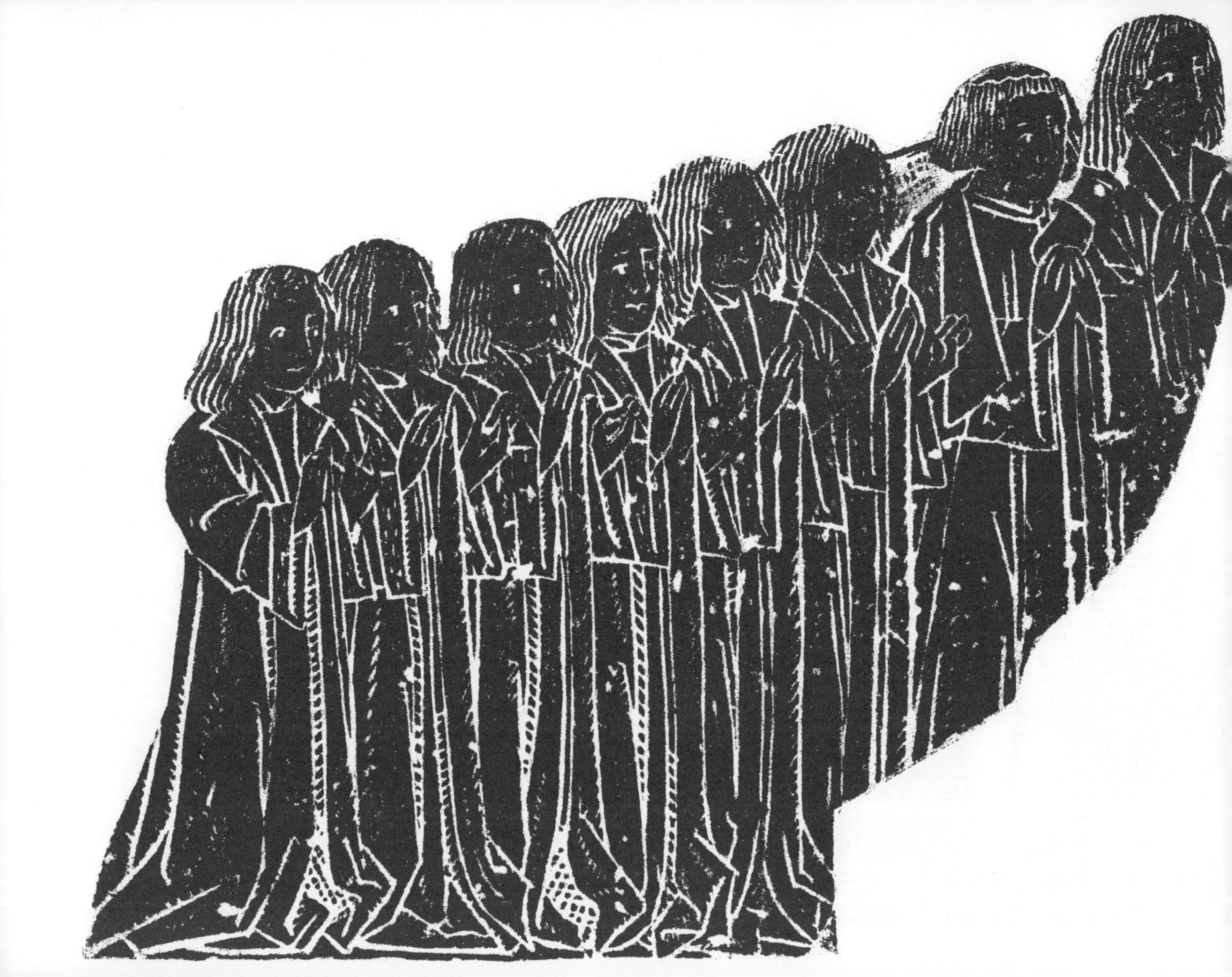

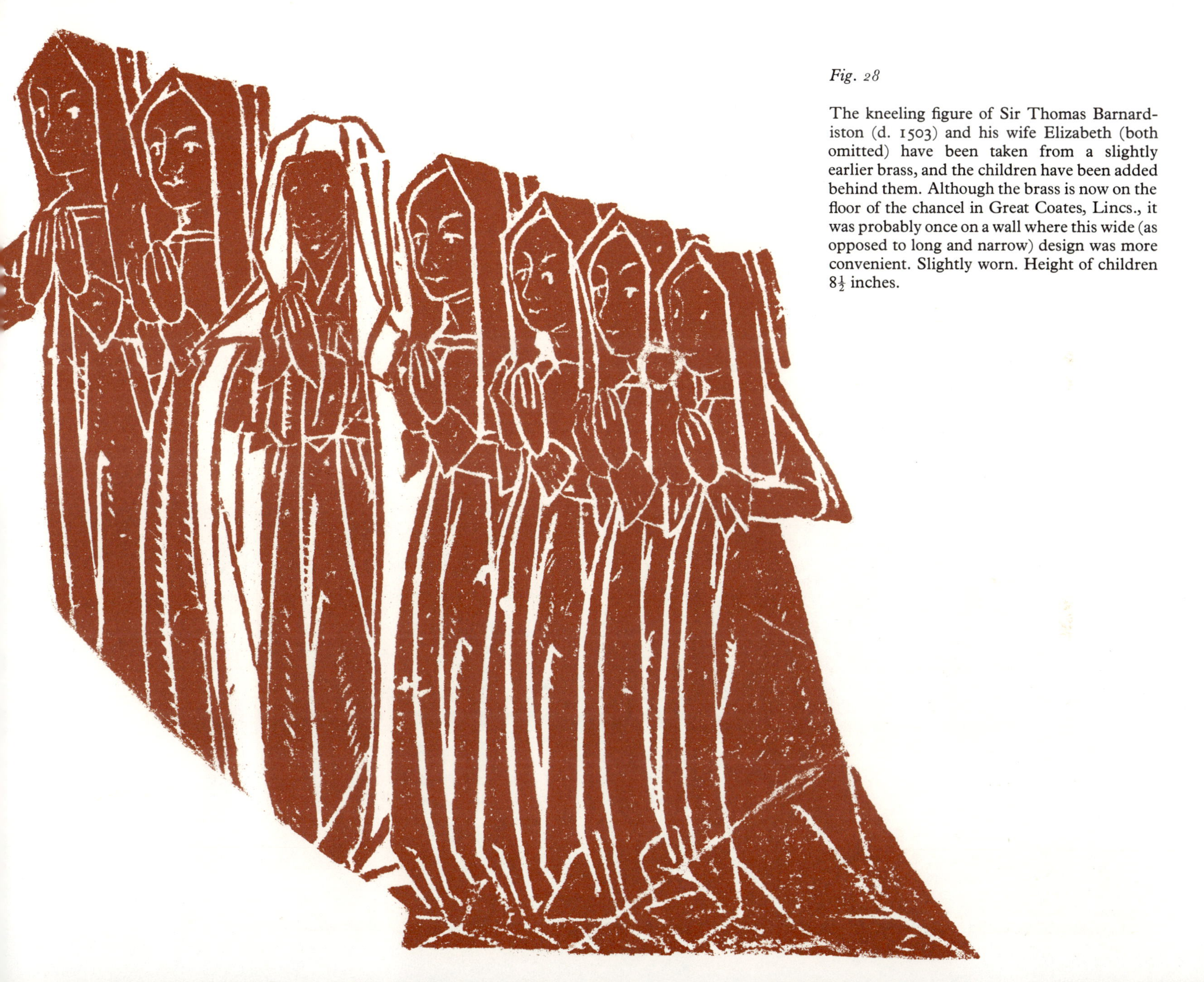

Fig. 28

The kneeling figure of Sir Thomas Barnardiston (d. 1503) and his wife Elizabeth (both omitted) have been taken from a slightly earlier brass, and the children have been added behind them. Although the brass is now on the floor of the chancel in Great Coates, Lincs., it was probably once on a wall where this wide (as opposed to long and narrow) design was more convenient. Slightly worn. Height of children $8\frac{1}{2}$ inches.

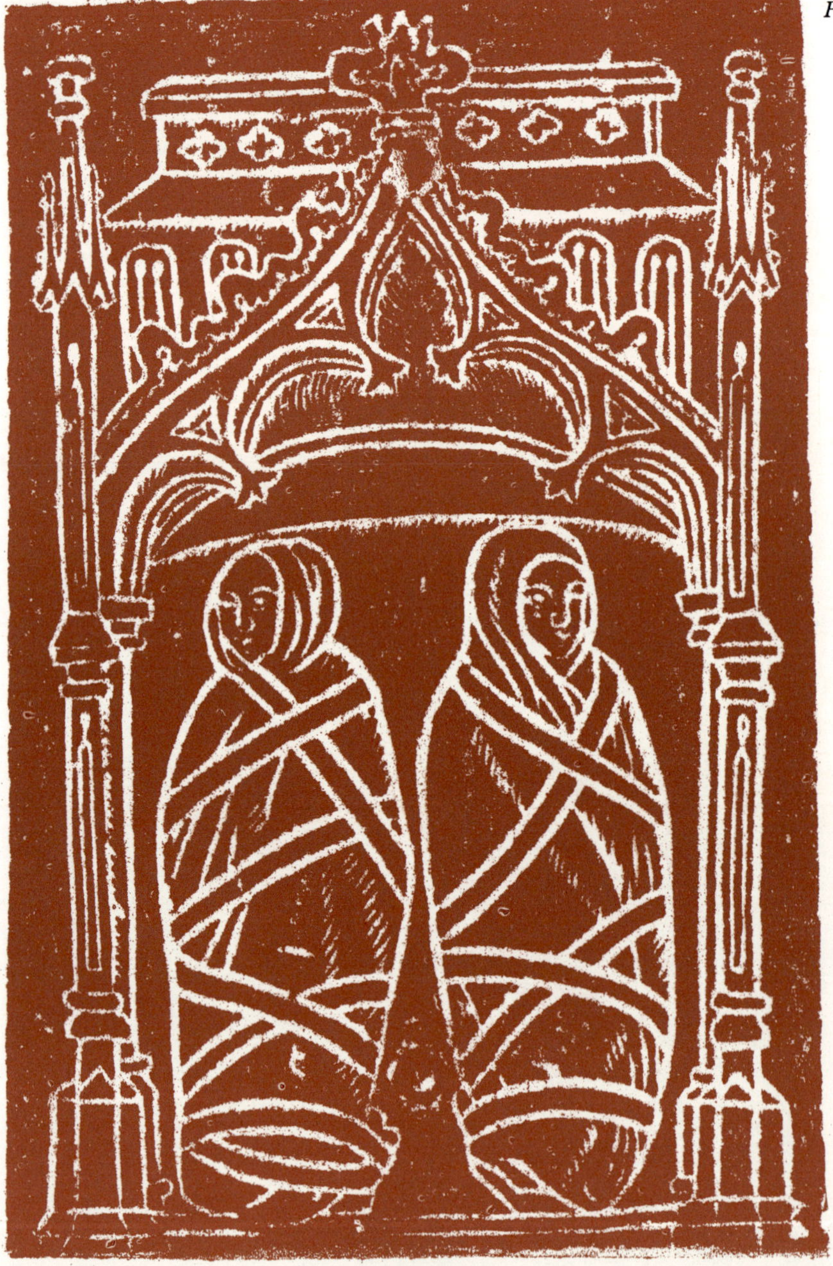

Fig. 29

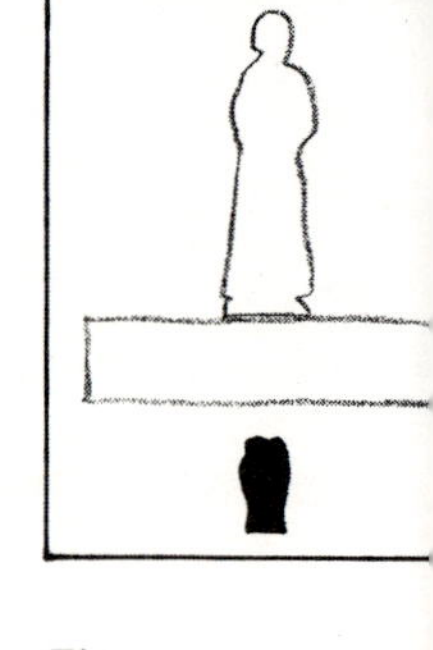

Fig. 30

ɡ. 29, *far left*

bies were swaddled (i.e. wound up in a sheet: see Joseph assisting Mary th this Fig. 3) for the first months of life. These two swaddled babies, hn (d. 1505) and Roger Yelverton (d. 1510) lie under a little canopy at ugham, Norfolk. Norfolk school work. Same scale.

ɡ. 30, *left*

is is the oddest pair, a little girl beside a swaddled baby her own height. ildren of Robert Heyward (d. 1509). Floor of south transept, Teynham, nt. Same scale.

ɡ. 31, *right*

ne à Wode was Thomas Astely's second wife and died in childbirth. e inscription states that the twins were a boy and a girl who, after a zardous birth, departed suddenly to the Lord on the day of St Agatha rtyr, in the year of our most bounteous Christ 1512. Note the zig-zag ing across the stomach (convenient for pregnancy?). The broad white rder of her gown and head dress are deeply recessed to take pigment. rfolk school. Nave floor, Blickling, Norfolk. Height 17 inches.

ɡ. 32, *far right*

rothy Parkinson, who also died in childbirth (1592), holds her twins chard and Marmaduke. Placed high on wall by pulpit, Haughton-le- erne, Durham. Height 17½ inches.

Fig. 31

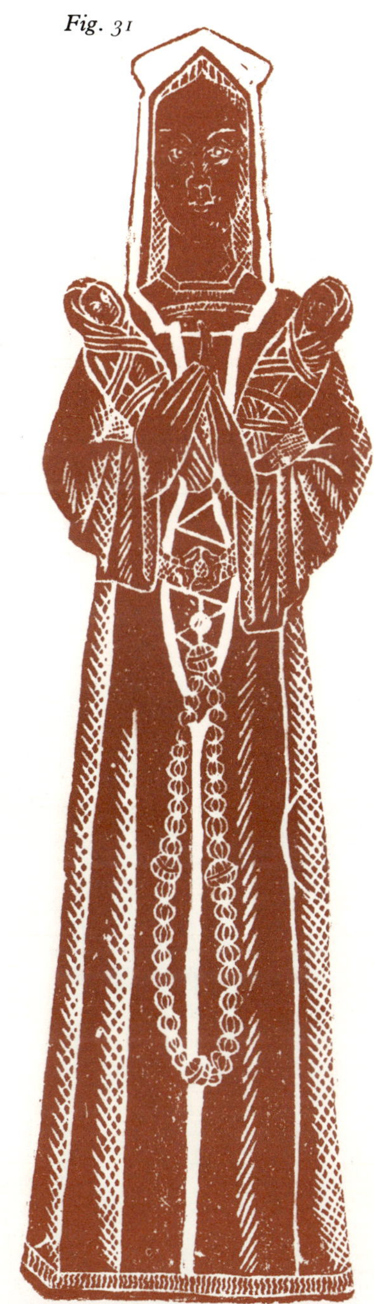

Fig. 32

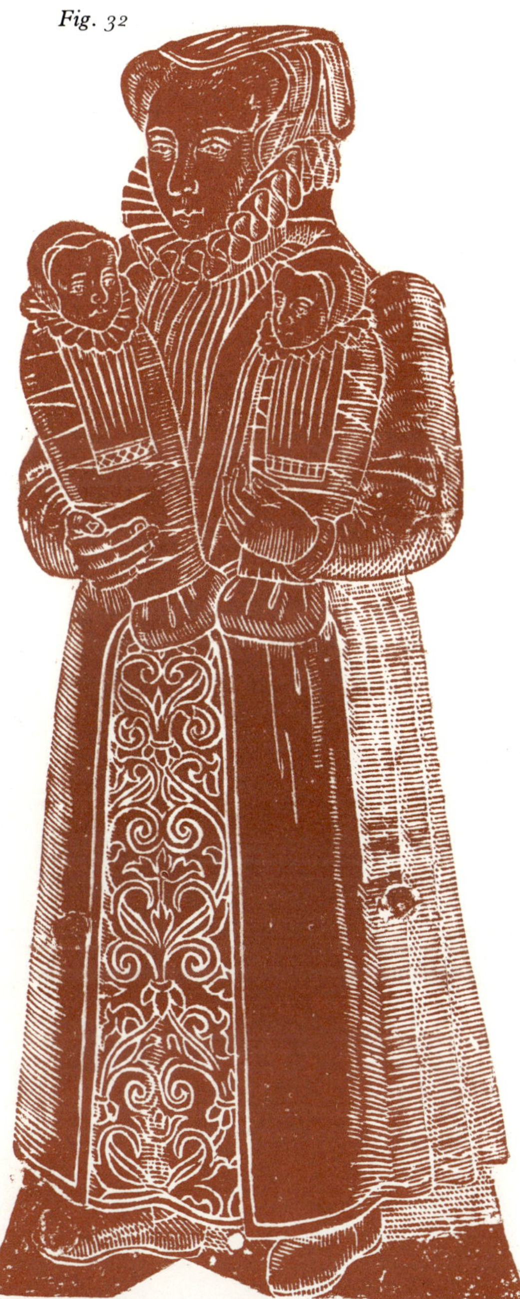

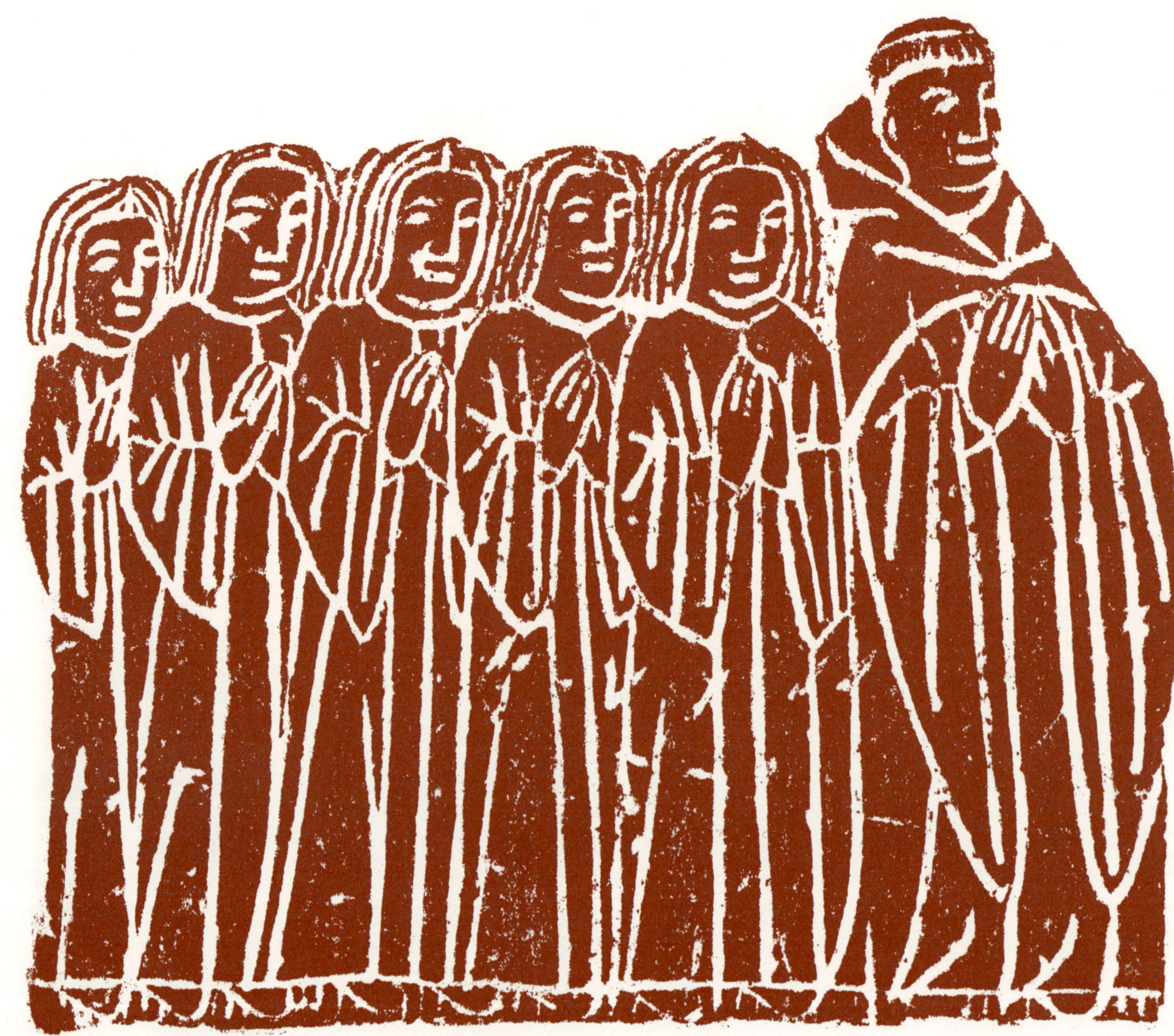

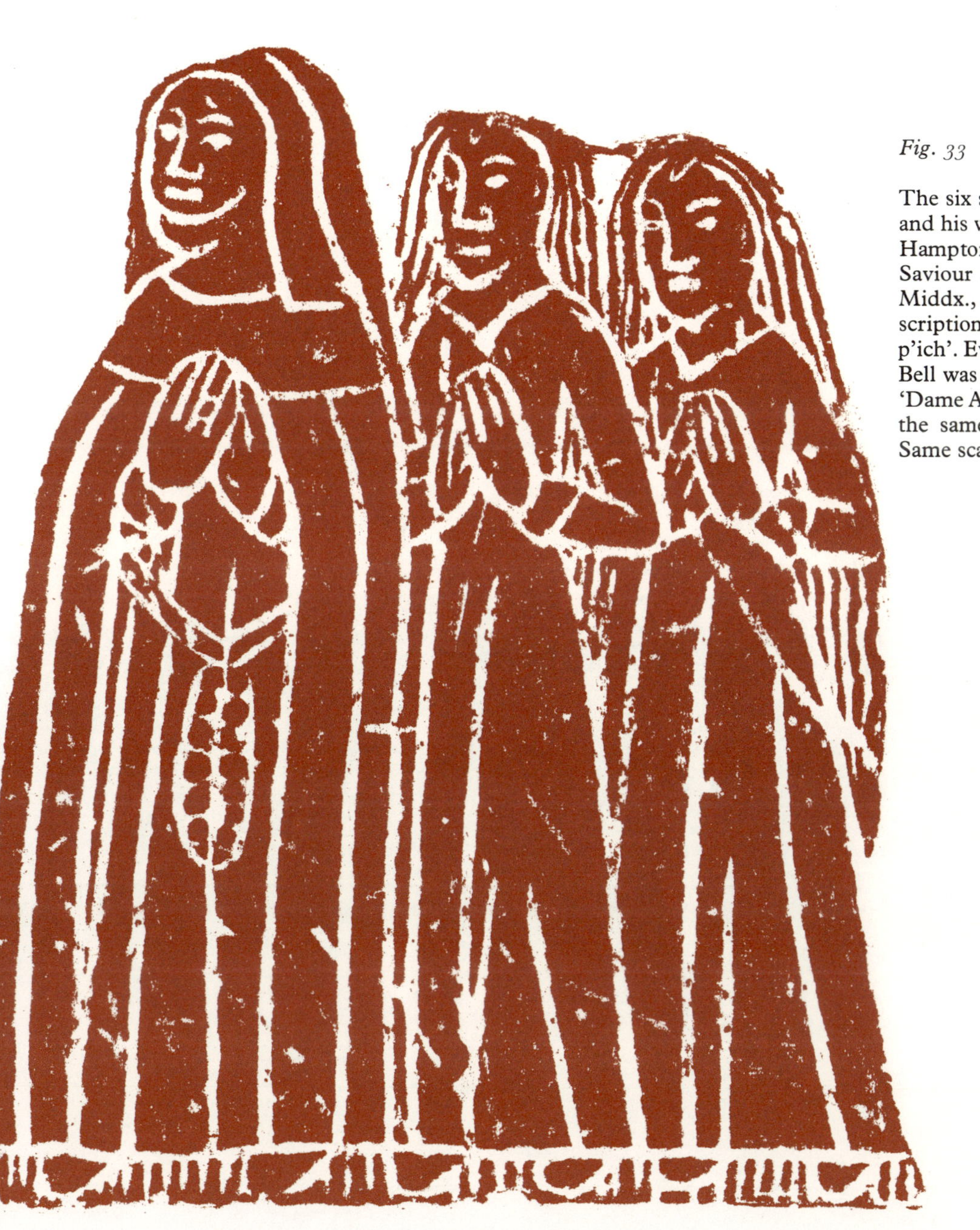

Fig. 33

The six sons and three daughters of John Hampton (d. 1556) and his wife Elyn are led in prayer by a monk and dame Alice Hampton. She was a Sister of the Chapter of the order of St Saviour and St Bridget whose house was at Syon, Isleworth, Middx., and was a great benefactor to the order. The inscription says that 'she was beneficiall to this church and p'ich'. Evidence of this was discovered in 1921 when a Sanctus Bell was recovered from Langford's Mill with the inscription 'Dame Alys Hampton, 1515'. The brass was engraved at about the same date. On wall of tower, Minchinhampton, Glos. Same scale.

Fig. 34

Dull monotonous engraving like this is found too often during the first half of the sixteenth century. Some people have mistakenly thought that smaller groups of children in this style record multiple births. Originally 25 children. The 9 sons have been stolen, but are reproduced from an old graphite dabbing in the Society of Antiquaries, London. Nave floor, Burnham, Bucks. Width of daughters 12 inches.

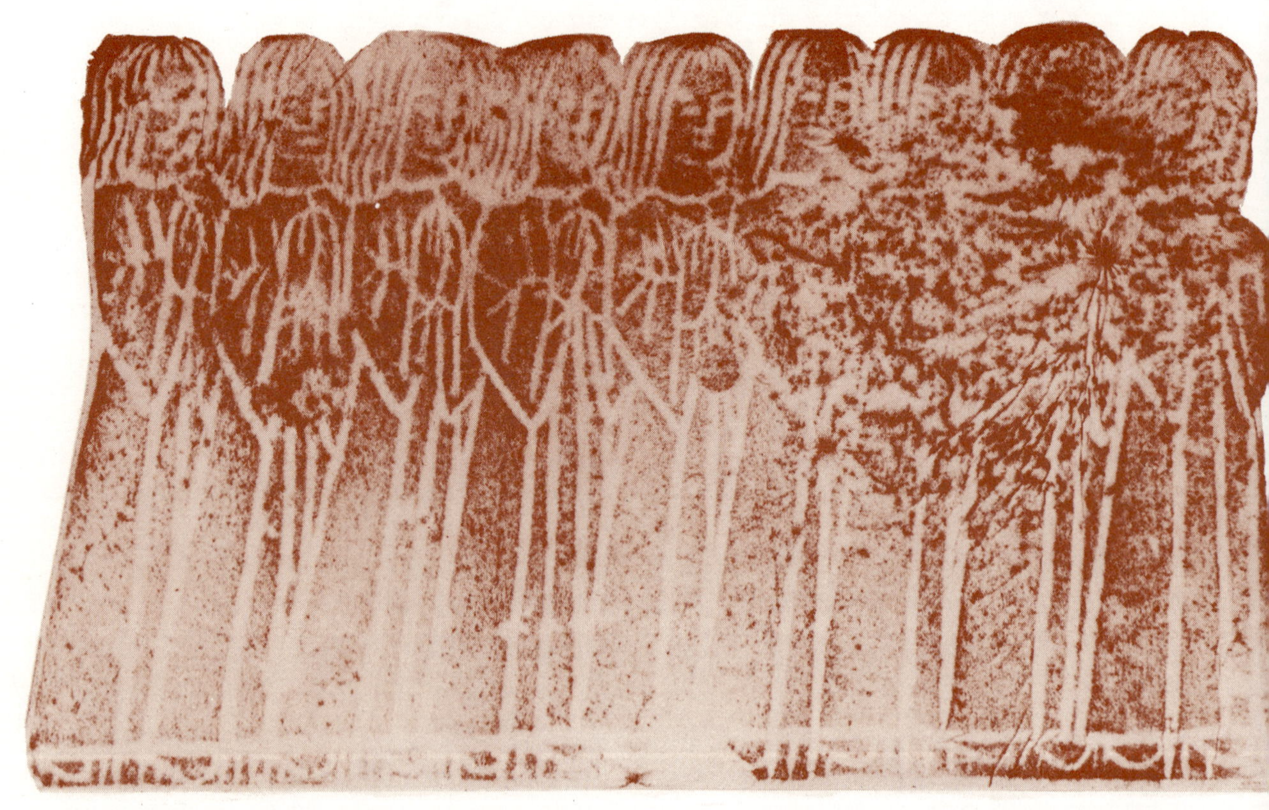

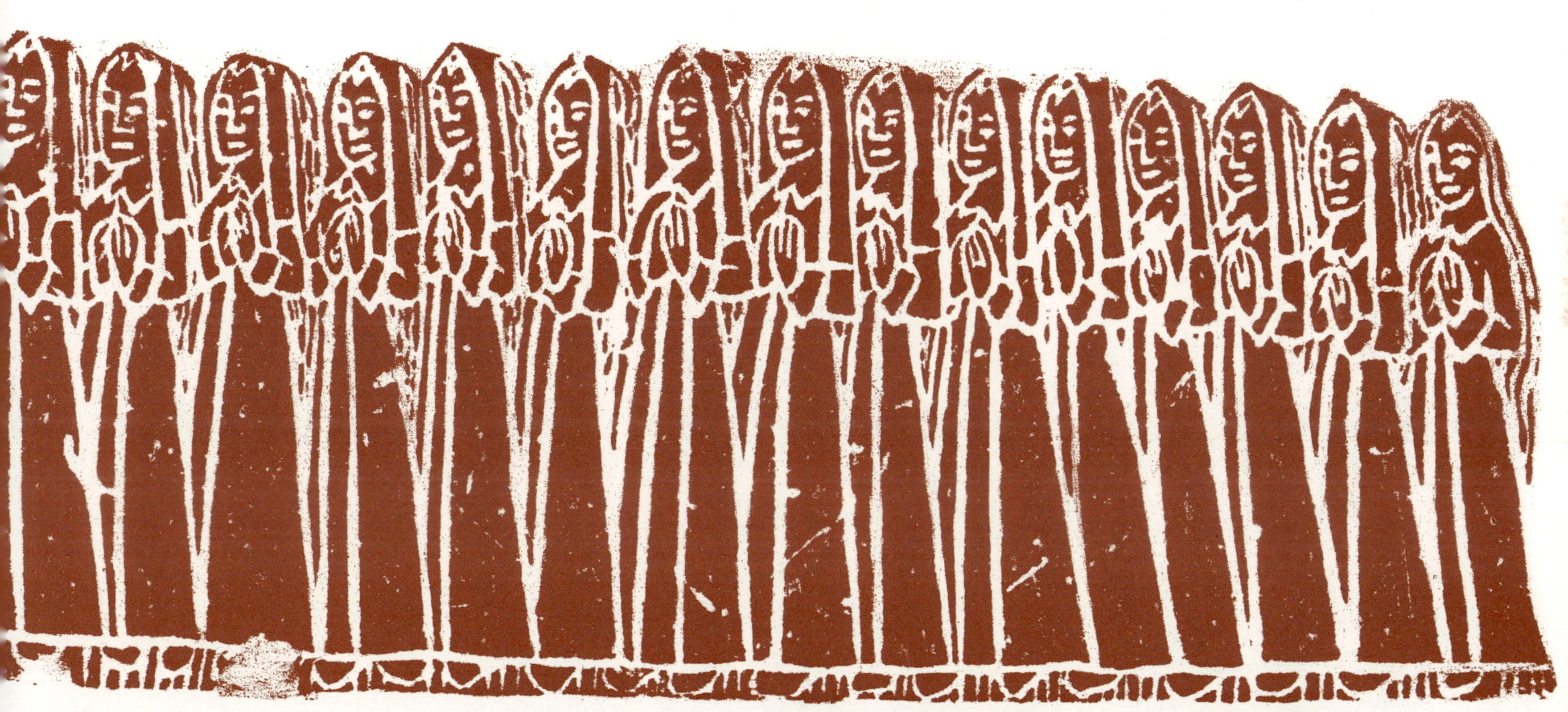

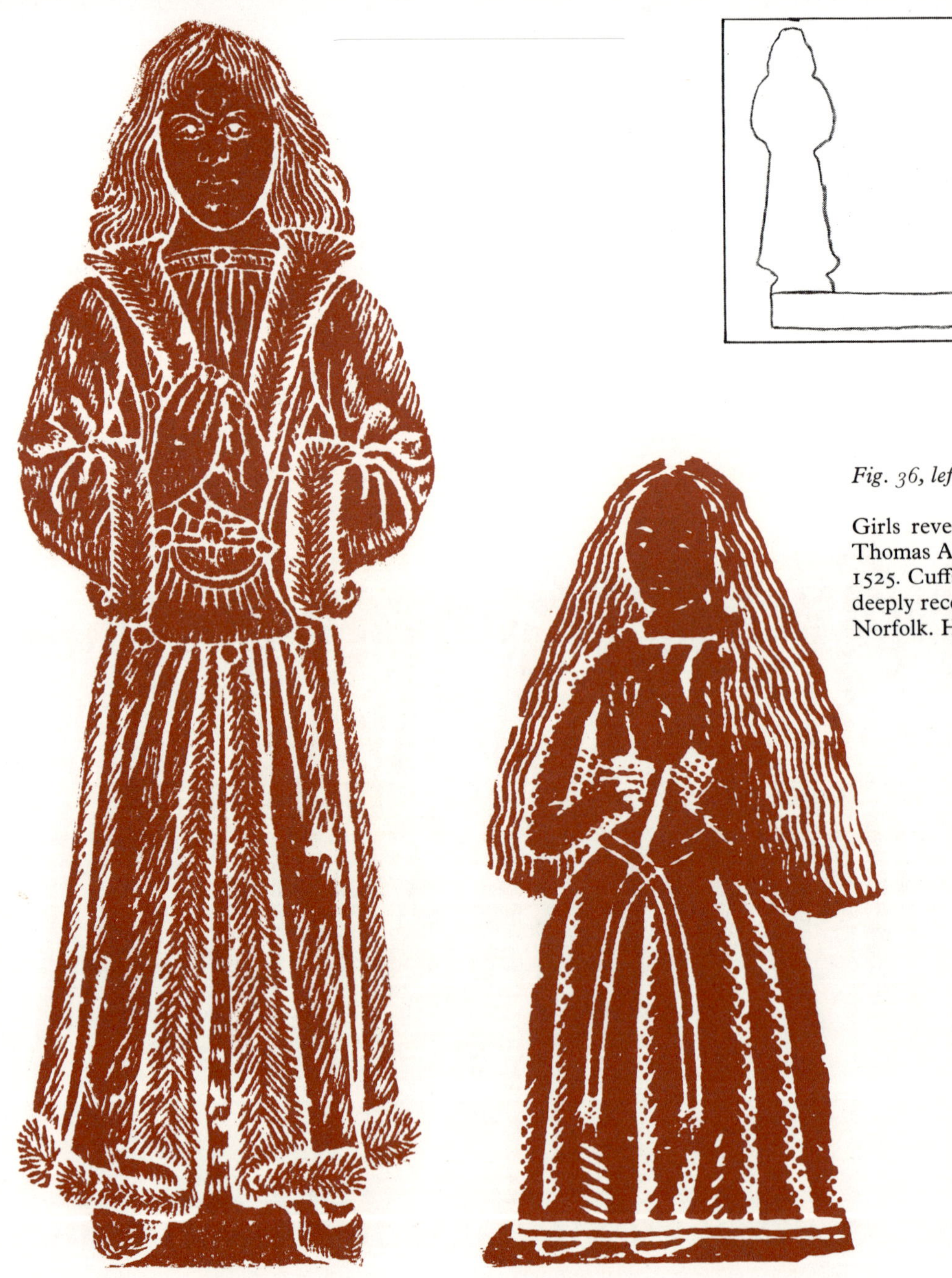

Fig. 35, far left

Boys and adults dressed alike. On a brass at Ditchingham, Norfolk, William is a miniature version of his father Philip Bozard (d. 1505), who stands beside him. Norfolk school, floor of choir. Height $11\frac{3}{4}$ inches.

Fig. 36, left

Girls reveal their youth by their long hair. Margaret was daughter of Thomas Aldriche, mayor of Norwich, and 'died in her floryshing youthe', 1525. Cuffs, hem, neck and the front line of her dress as far as the waist are deeply recessed to take pigment. Norfolk school. Floor of nave, Yelverton, Norfolk. Height $6\frac{1}{2}$ inches.

Figs. 37 and 38

Two children engraved in London: Wenefride (d. 1547), and her brother Richard Newport (d. 1551). She wears a puff-shouldered dress and he a gown with false sleeves. Floor of south aisle, Greystoke, Cumberland. Height of boy 11½ inches.

Fig. 39, next page

A slightly worn group of sons (one son and five badly worn daughters omitted) from Radnage, Bucks. They hold books or rosaries and seven of the eight have names below. One son is a priest. Children of William (d. 1534), and Sebell Este. On wall of nave. Width 11 inches.

Fig. 37

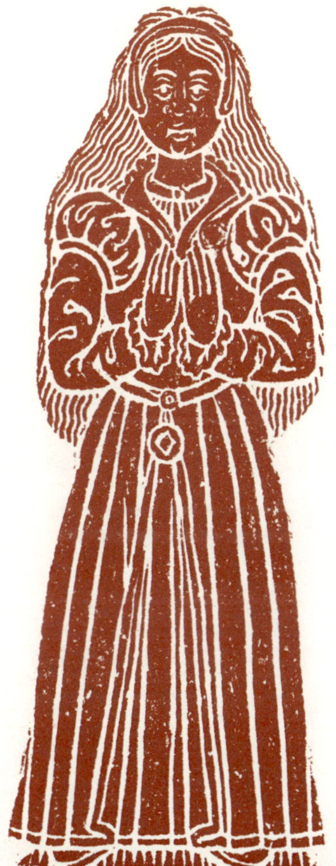

Fig. 38

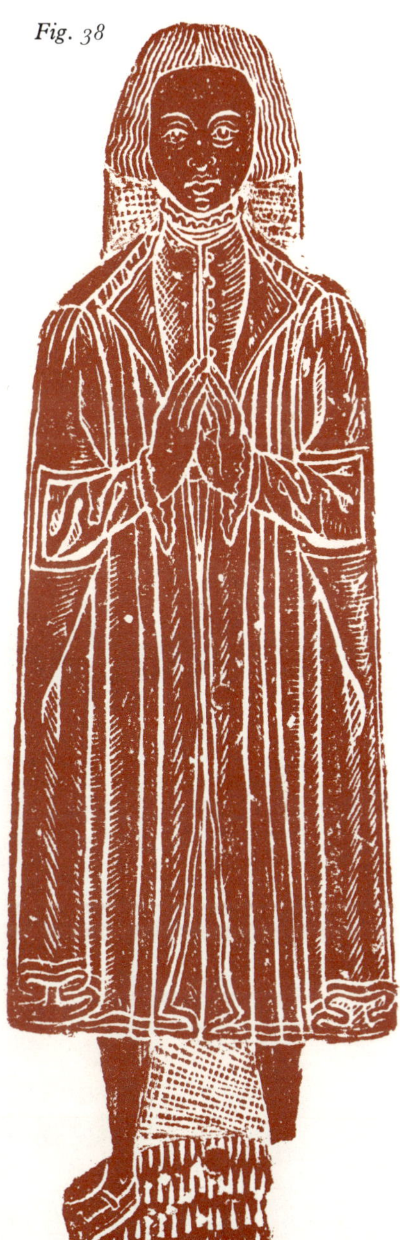

Fig. 39

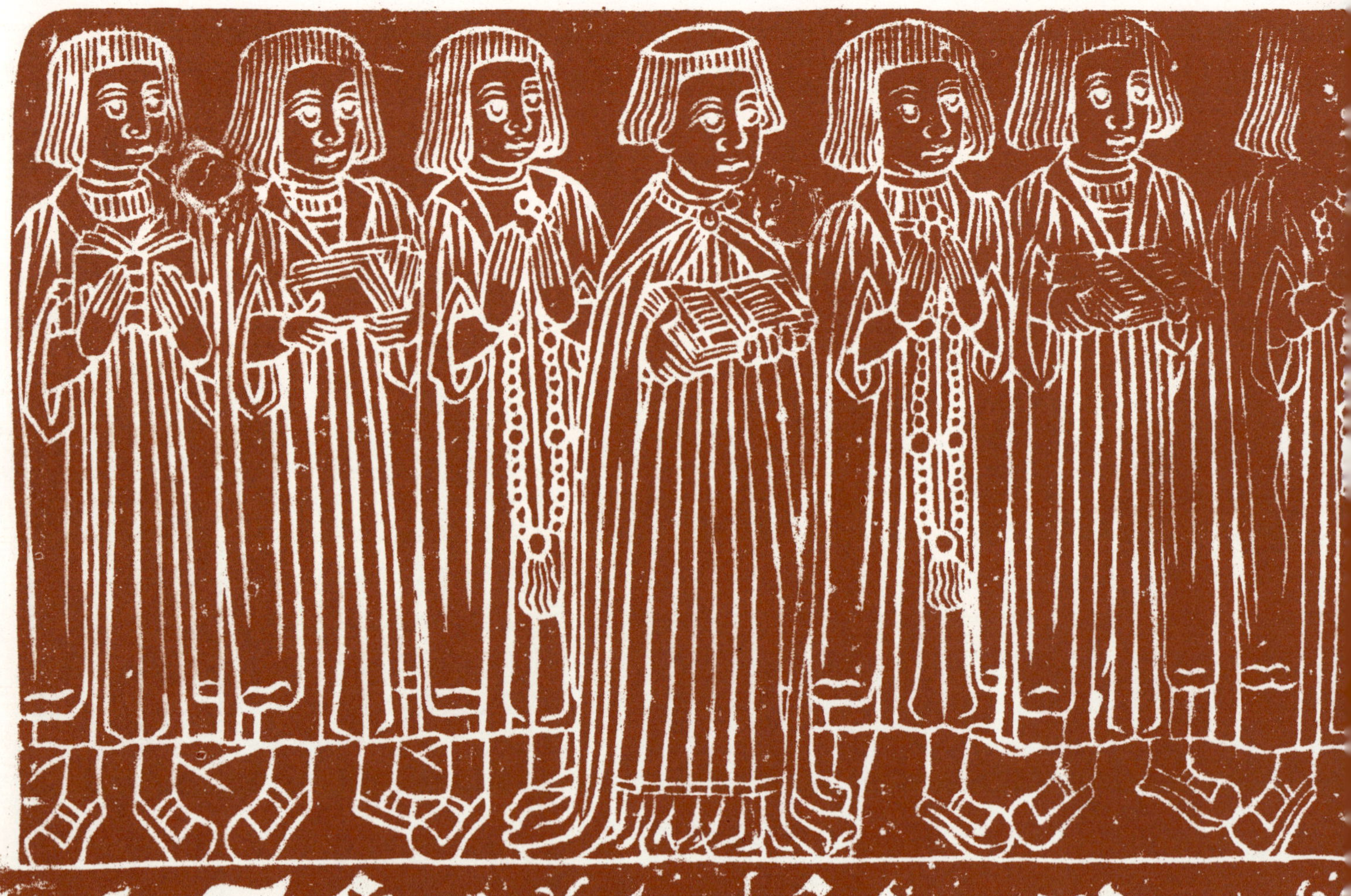

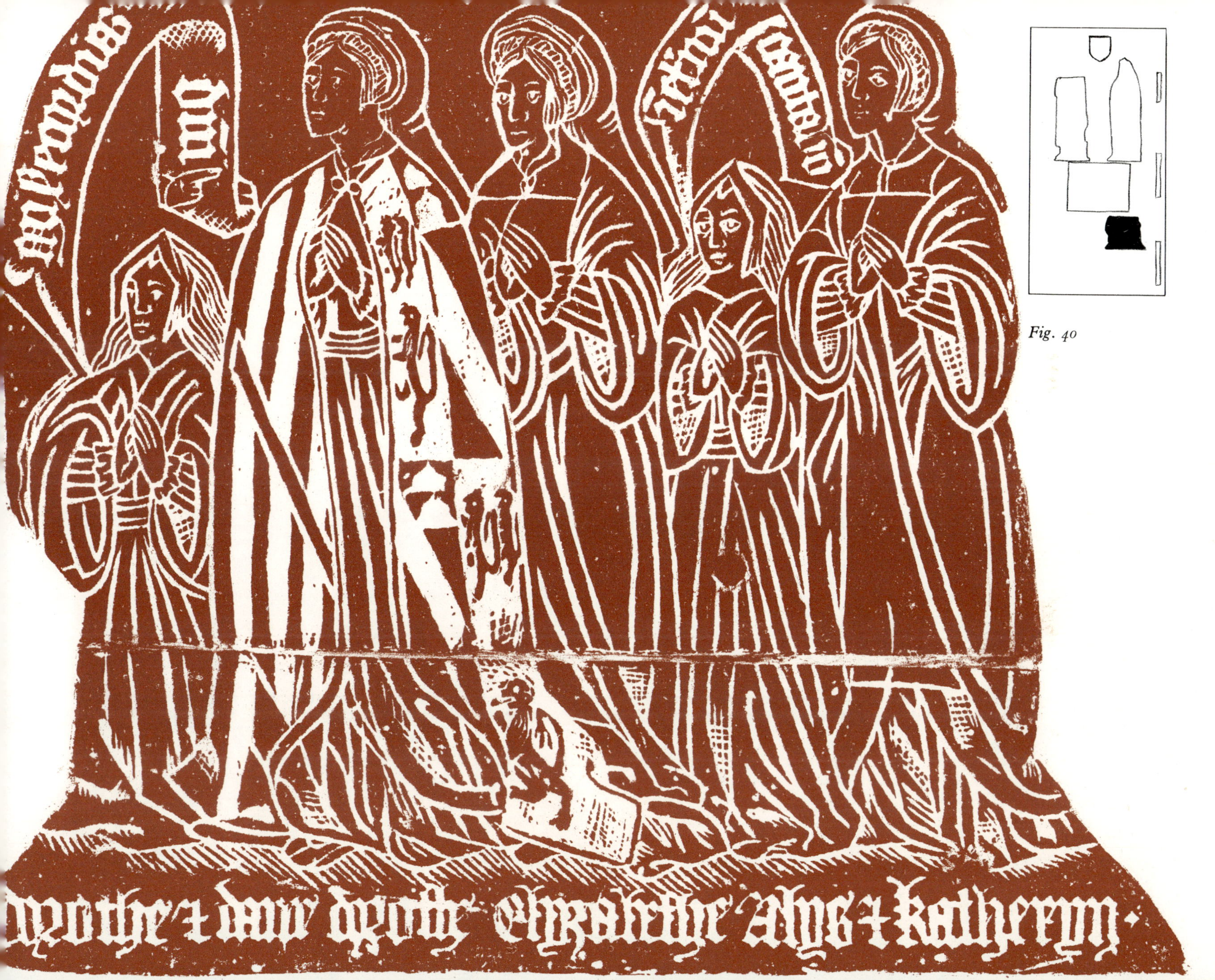

Fig. 40

Fig. 40, previous page

'Dorothe and Dame Dorothe, Elysabethe, Alys and Katheryn' were daughters of Sir Anthony Fitzherbert (1470–1538) by his second wife Maud. Sir Anthony was knighted and made a judge of the common pleas in 1522. He signed articles of impeachment against Wolsey. His '*La Graunde Abridgment*' was the first significant attempt to systematize the whole law. Dame Dorothe married Sir Ralph Longford and she wears her father's arms; Fitzherbert, *gu. 3 lions rampant or.* quartering Fitzherbert, *arg. a chief vairy or & gu. over all a bend sa.* on her left, and her husband's *paly or. & gu. a bend arg.* on her right. On floor of chancel, Norbury, Derbyshire. Width 15 inches.

Dame Dorothe afterwards married Sir John Porte (d. 1557) of Etwall, Derbyshire, and appears there on a brass as his second wife wearing another heraldic mantle.

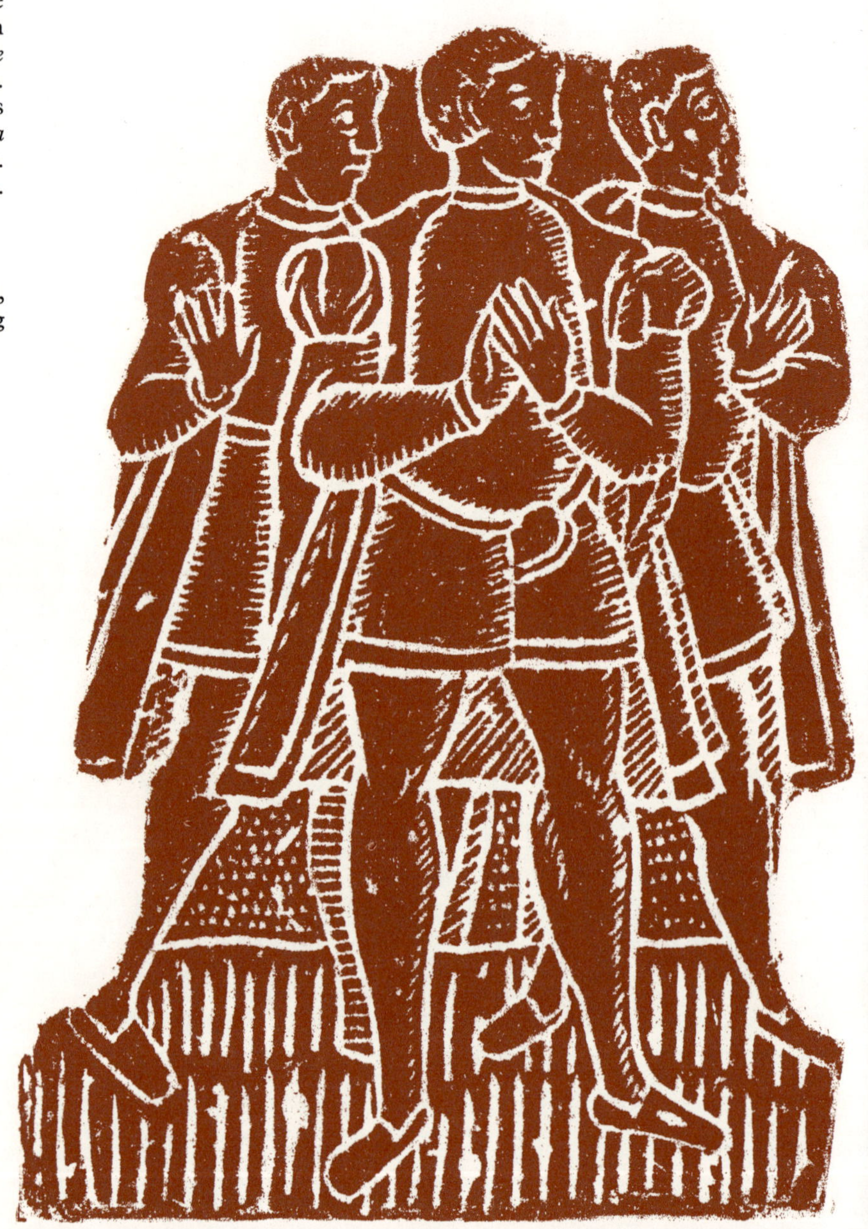

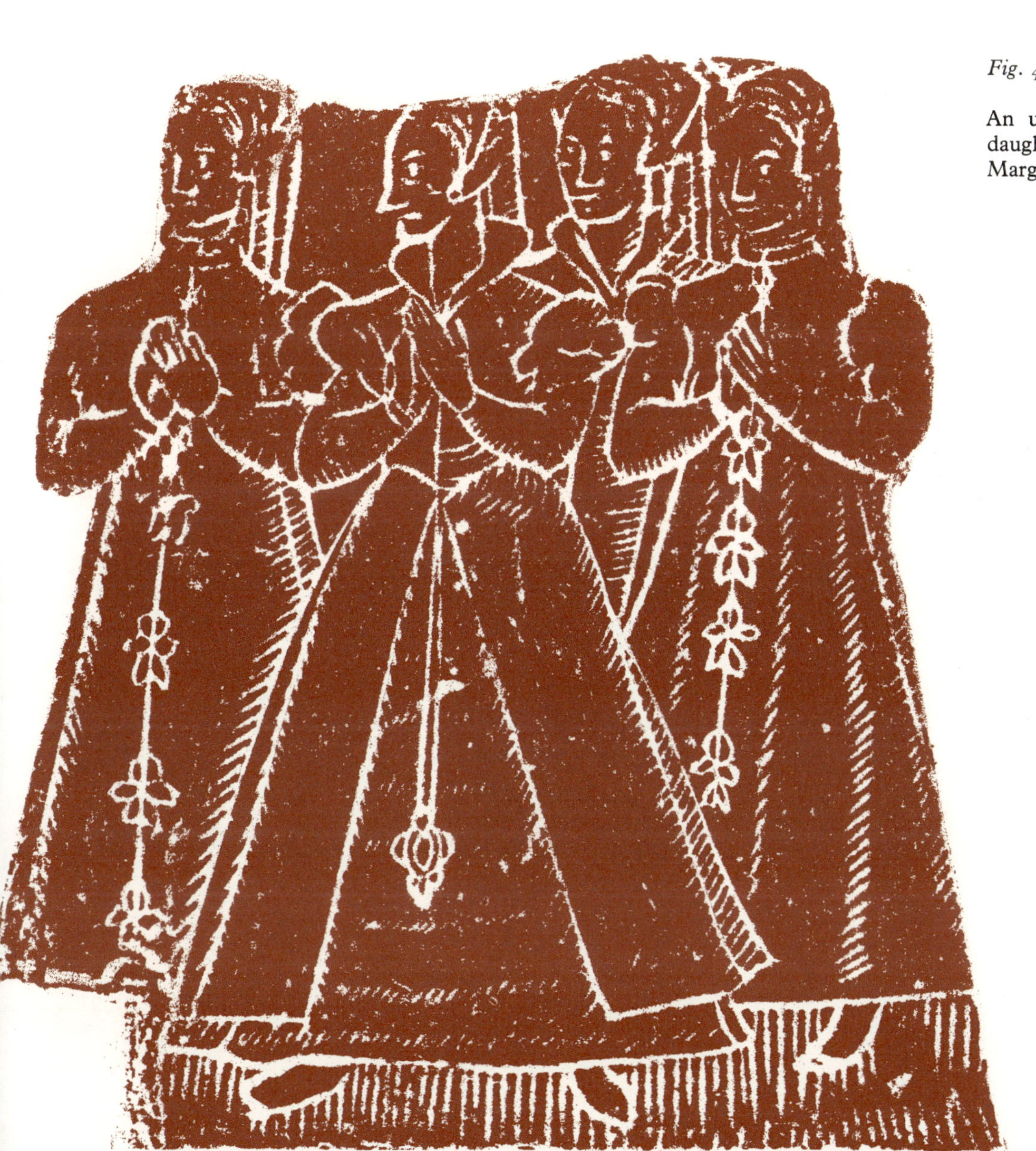

Fig. 41, left

An unusually lively group of three sons and four daughters (*c.* 1550), parents unknown. Chancel wall, Margaretting, Essex. Same scale.

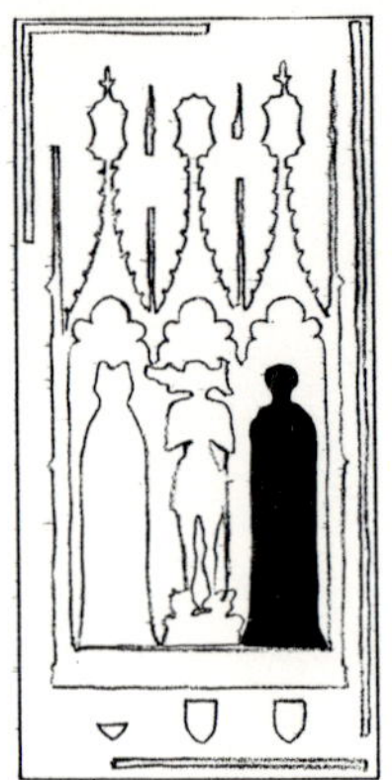

Fig. 42

At the dissolution of the monasteries and chantry chapels around 1537 many brasses were sold as scrap metal. The large figure of a lady of 1447 was turned over and engraved in about 1538 with a group of thirteen children on three levels. It seems a remarkably ugly arrangement. The brass was stolen in 1898 and recovered in fifty-five pieces after it had been broken up for the melting pot. The remains are on the wall, Okeover, Staffordshire.

Near right. Before the theft.

Far right. The earlier side after recovery.

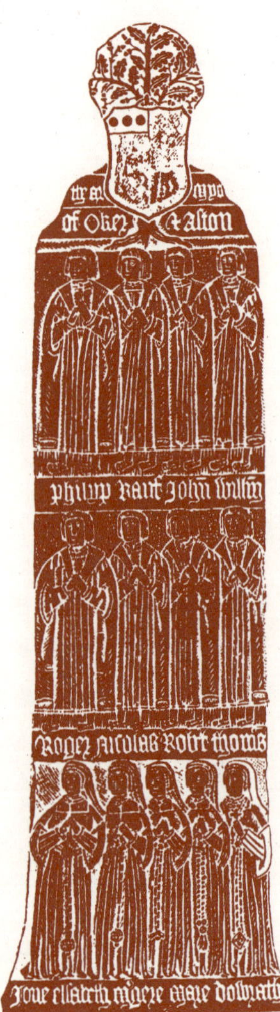

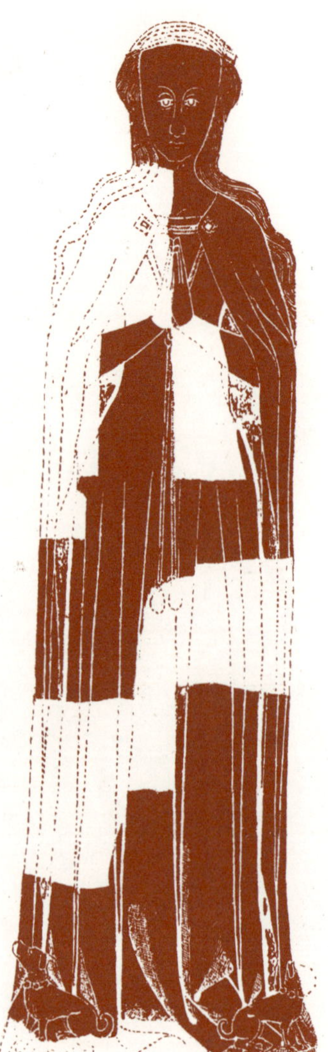

Fig. 43

Figs. 40 and 42 have been engraved on the backs of earlier brasses. In simple contrast to Fig. 42 this small figure in a furred gown (*c.* 1520) has been turned over to create a boy in a shorter gown (*c.* 1540). Archaeological and Ethnographical Museum, Downing Street, Cambridge. Height 7¾ inches.

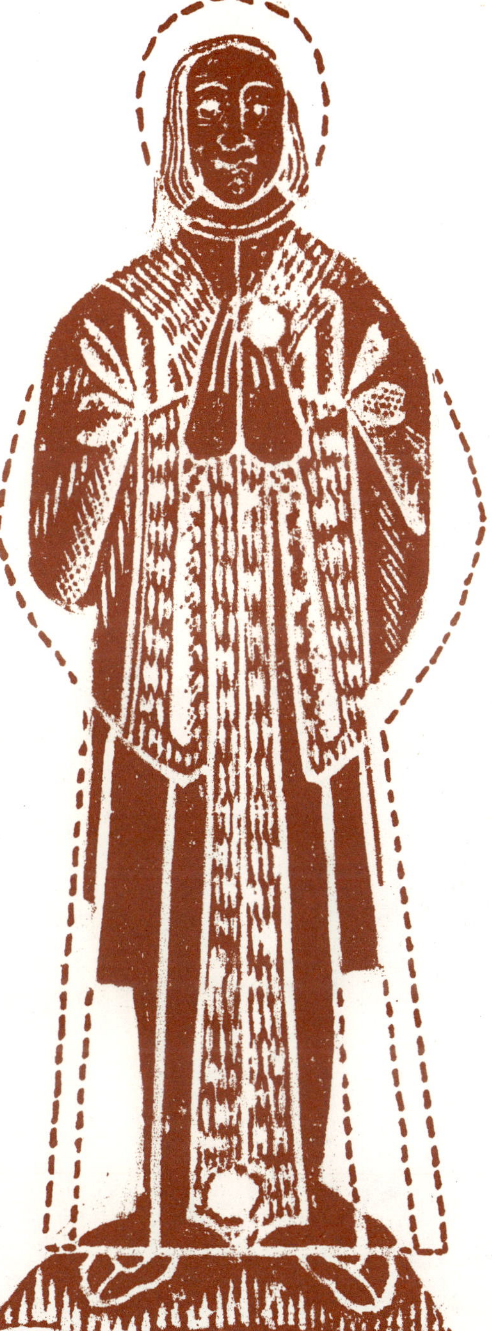

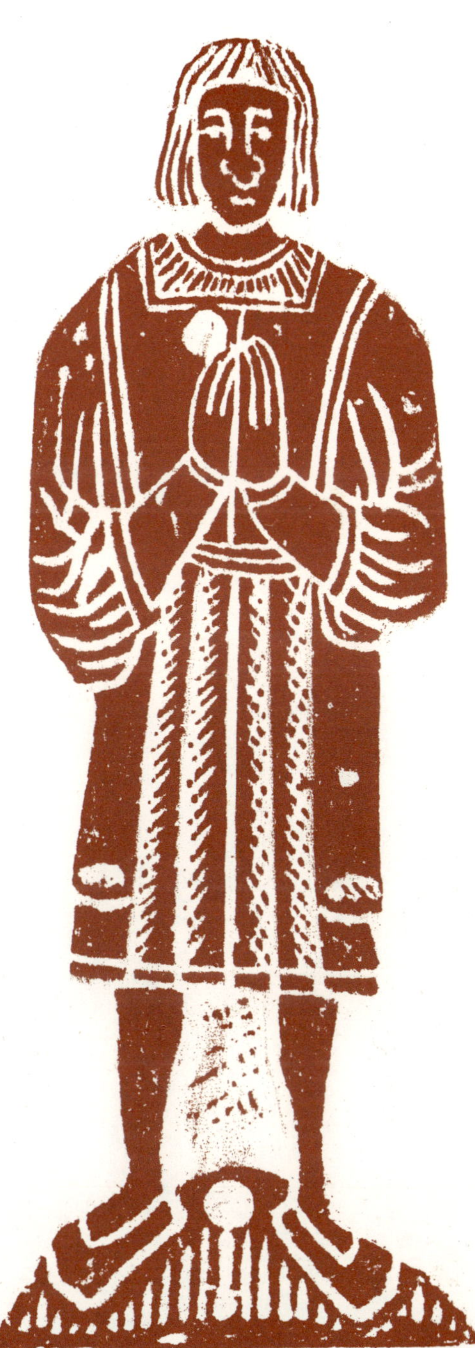

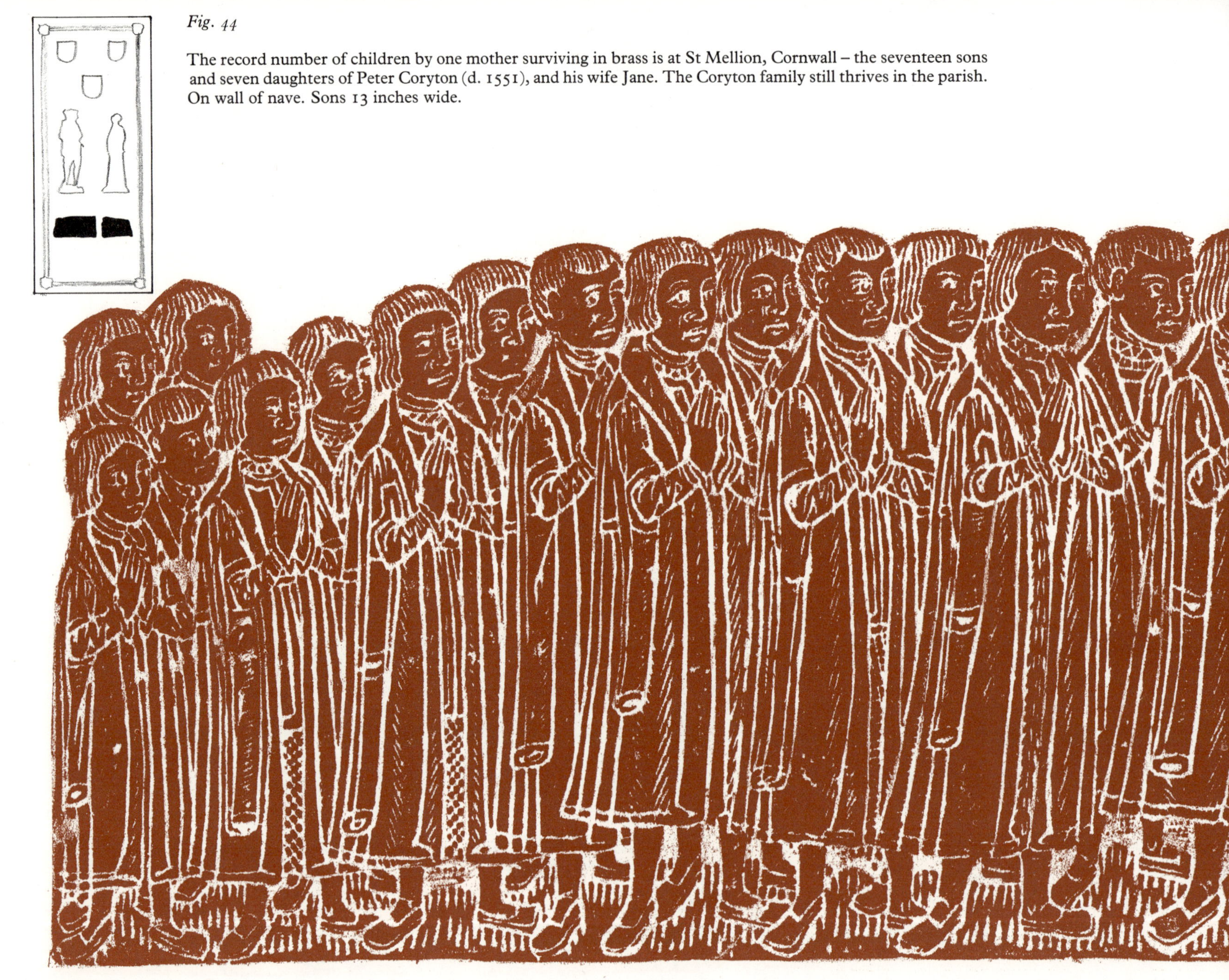

Fig. 44

The record number of children by one mother surviving in brass is at St Mellion, Cornwall – the seventeen sons and seven daughters of Peter Coryton (d. 1551), and his wife Jane. The Coryton family still thrives in the parish. On wall of nave. Sons 13 inches wide.

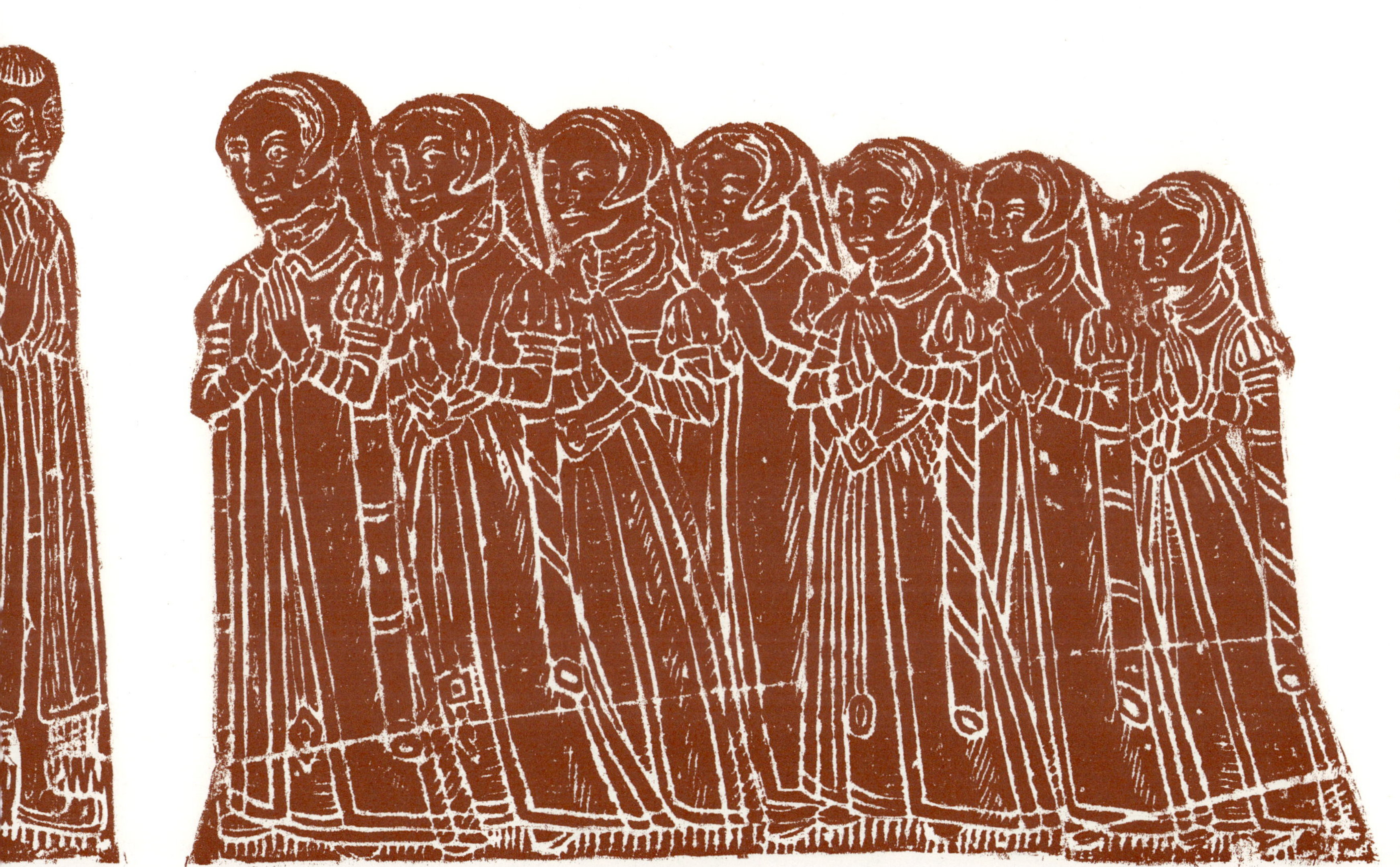

Fig. 45

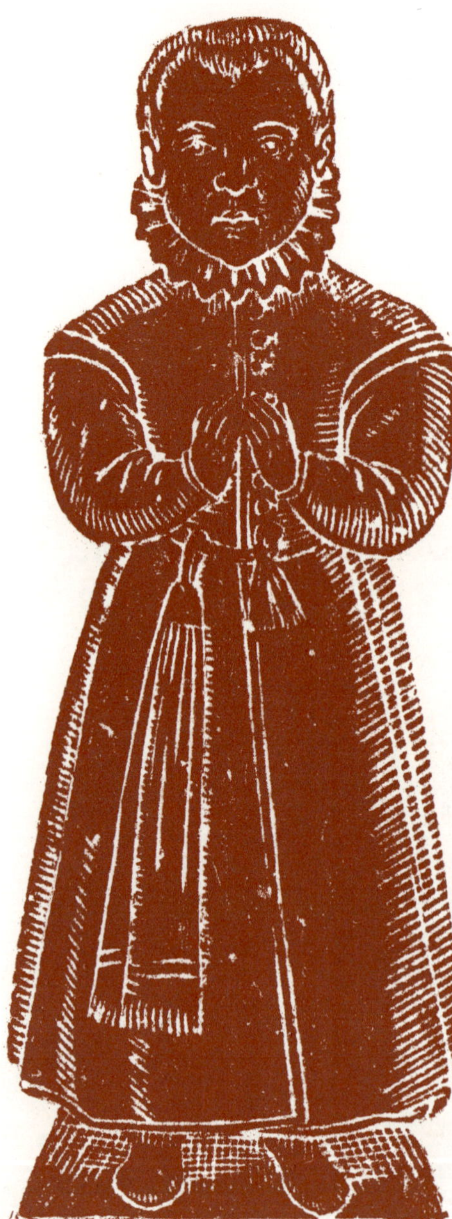

Fig. 46

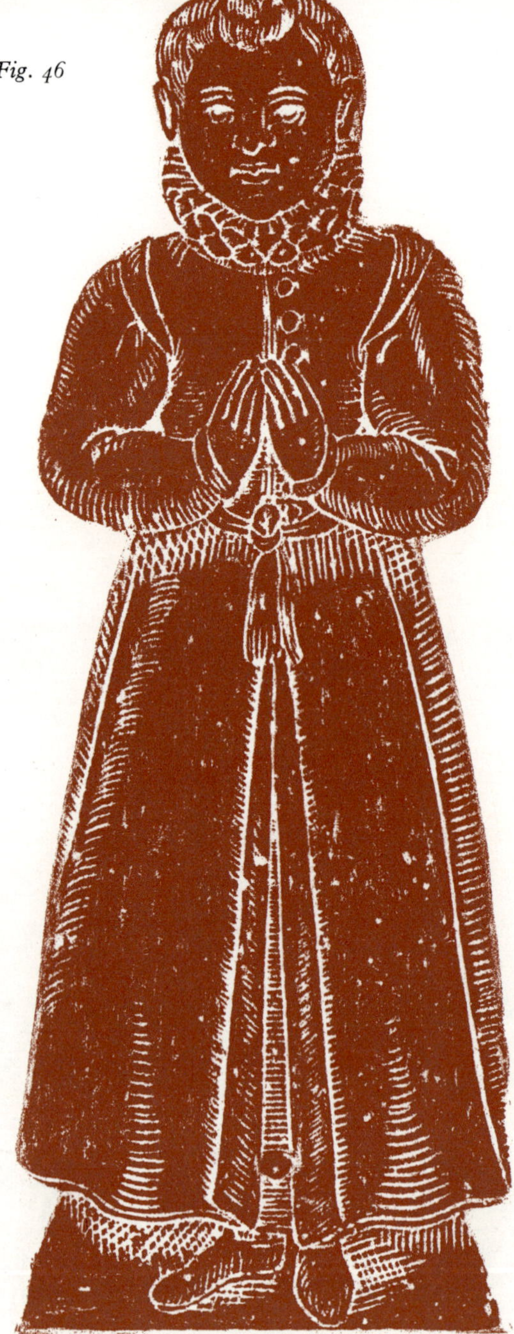

Figs. 45, 46

Richard Best, *far left*, (d. 1587), Merstham, Surrey, and Nathaniel Bacon, *left* (Fig. 46, d. 1588), Essex, aged three, are similar London-made figures. The scarf hanging from Richard's waist probably serves as a handkerchief. Richard $9\frac{1}{4}$ inches and Nathaniel $10\frac{3}{4}$ inches.

Fig. 47

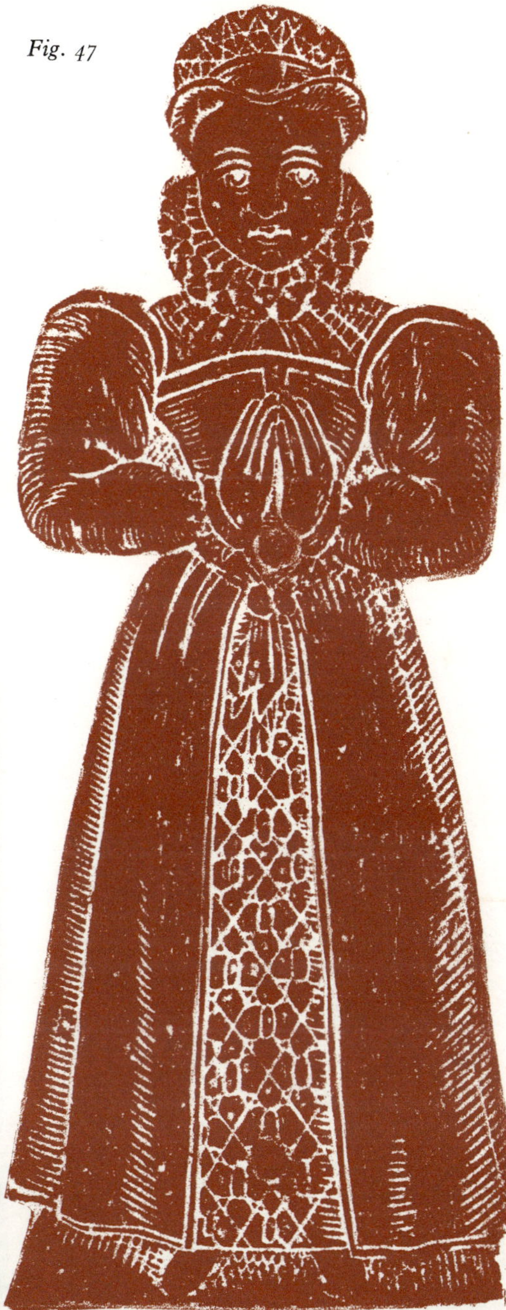

Fig. 48

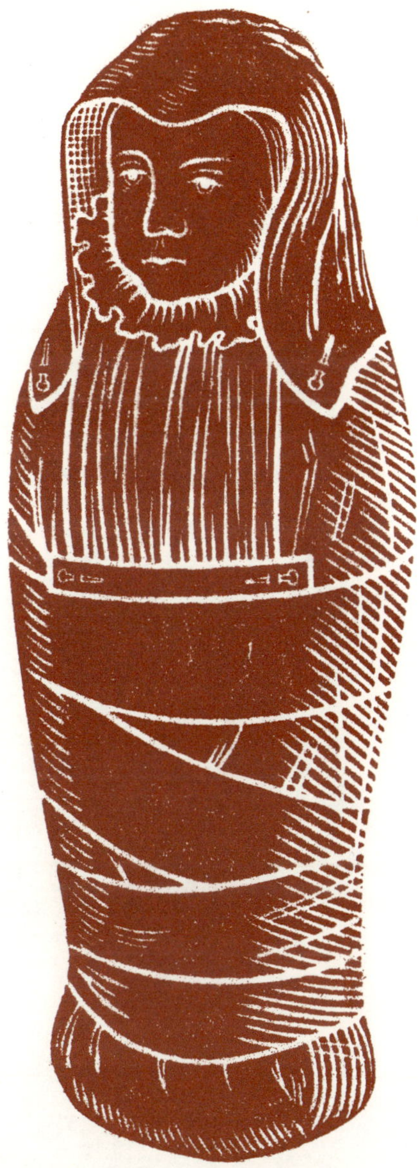

Fig. 47

Elizabeth Bacon *left* (d. 1588, aged two) chancel floor, Aveley, Essex. Height 10 inches.

Fig. 48

Peter Best *right* in pinned swaddling clothes was stolen *c.* 1860 and the rubbing is from a copy placed in Merstham, Surrey, in 1911. On wall of south aisle. Height 8 inches.

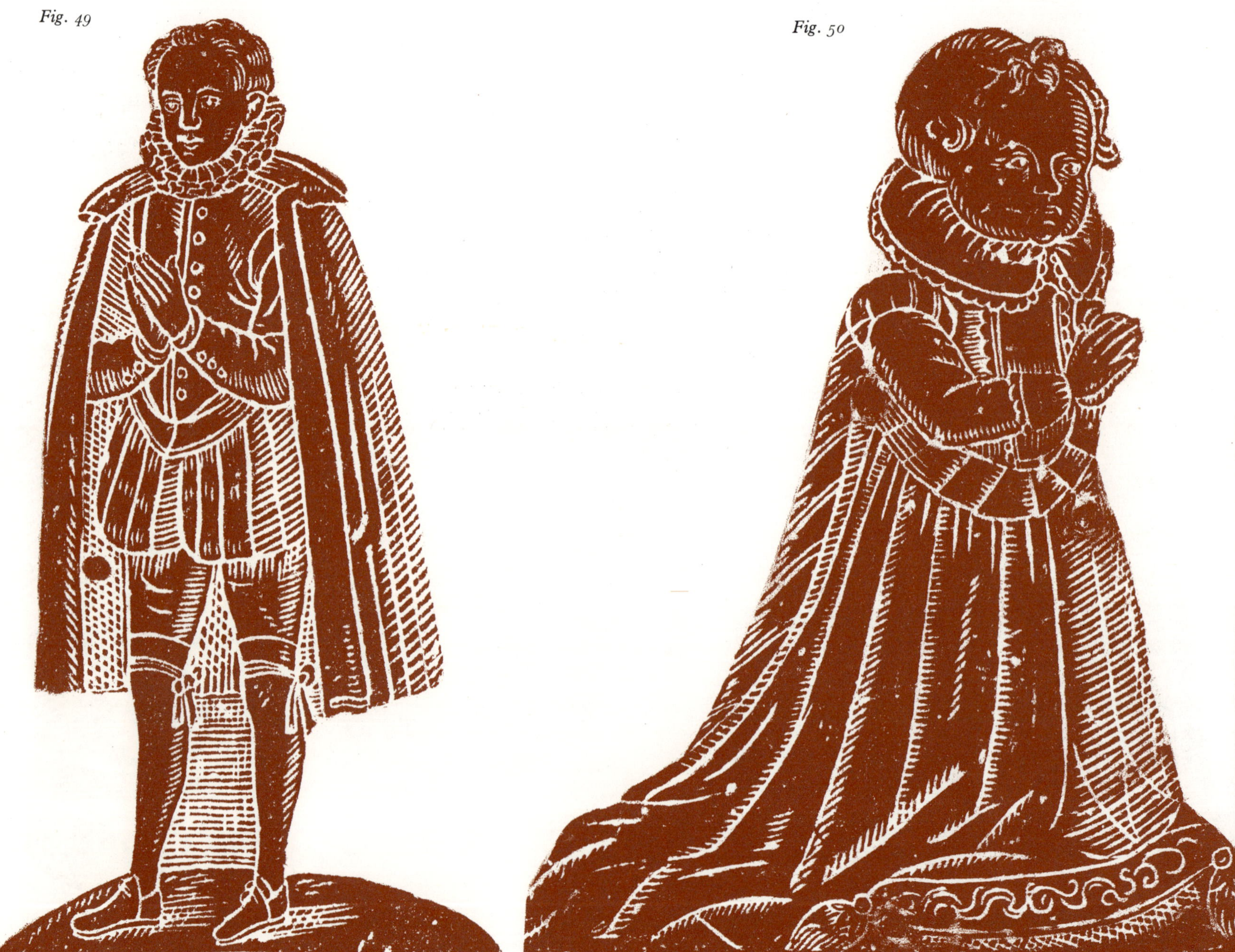

Fig. 49

Fig. 50

Fig. 51

Fig. 49, facing far left

William Brome (d. 1599, aged 10). He wears a doublet, cape and ruff like any adult. On wall of south transept, Holton, Oxon. The brass is only $8\frac{1}{2}$ inches high.

Fig. 50, left

John Drake (d. 1623), son of Francis Drake of Esher, Surrey, has an unusually childlike face for a brass. He died aged four. Floor of Drake Chapel, Amersham, Bucks. Height $10\frac{1}{4}$ inches.

Fig. 51, right

Thomas Tompkins was a little boy who died in a muddy pool in 1629. A Latin inscription tells how water preserved him as an infant (baptism) but how it drowned him as a boy. Thus twice washed he was unclean but now without sinking he will be washed for ever in the Blood of Christ. On wall of chancel, Llandinabo, Herefordshire. Same scale.

Me prius infantem servavit pura renatum,
Postea me puerum turbida mersit aqua :
Sic bis lotus eram fœdus, sed nunc sine labe,
Ablutus Christi sanguine semper ero.

The 'T' hanging on a cord round his neck is both monogram and cross.

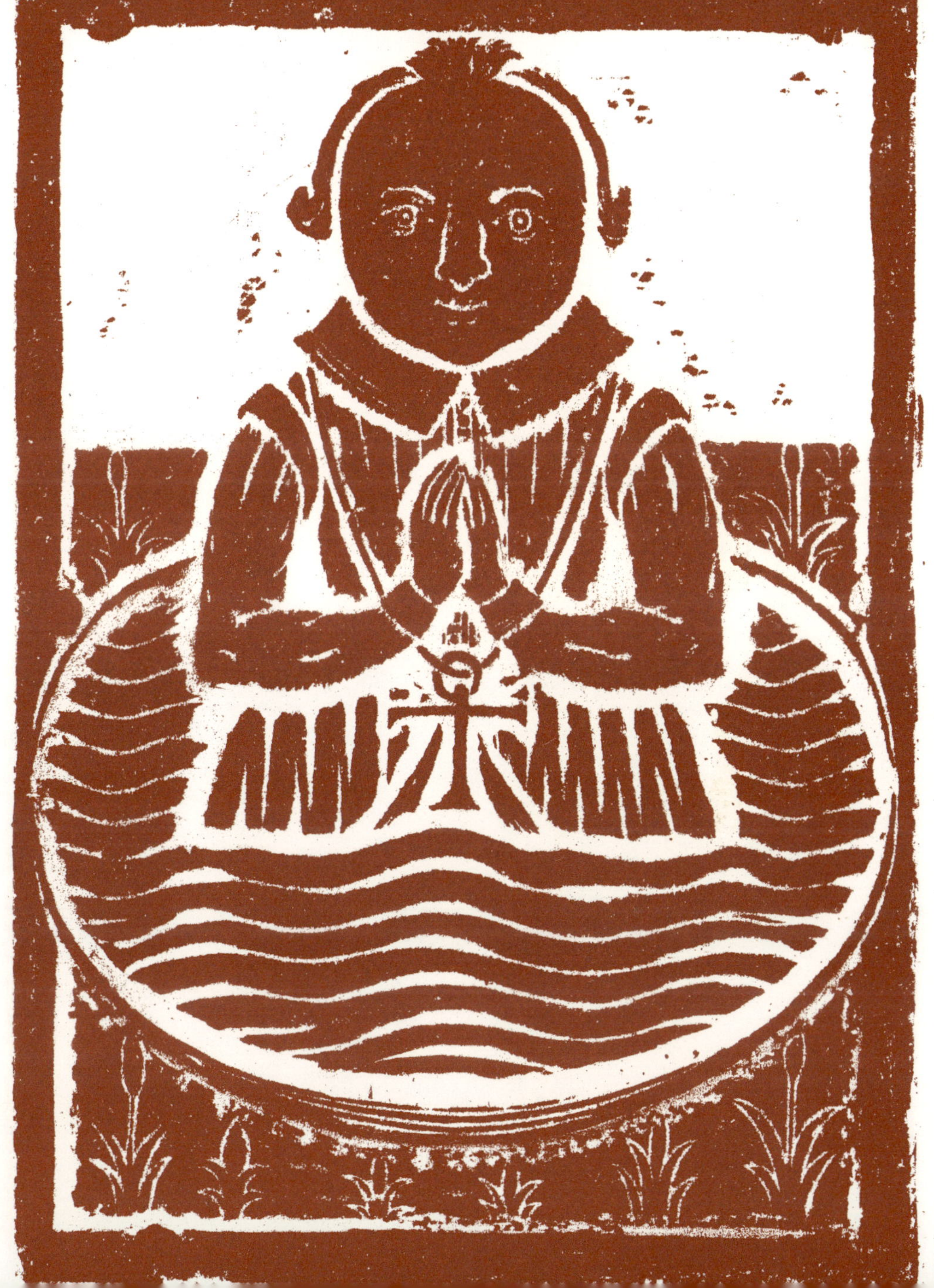

Fig. 52

The parade of 2 sons and 10 daughters of William Clerke (d. 1611) has been given a three-dimensional effect by means of a tiled floor. The perspective has been worked out with a vanishing point just off the top dexter corner. The rules of perspective explored by Italian painters of the fifteenth century only reached English brasses at about this time. Floor of nave, Wrotham, Kent. Same scale.

Fig. 53, next page left

Ann Savage, who died in childbirth, 1605, aged twenty-five, is shown in a four-poster bed, her swaddled baby, who lived, lying on the cover. The inscription suggests she was like the Phoenix dying to give life to her offspring: *'Velut altera Phoenix dum parit illa perit, dum parturit, interit Anna'*. On south wall of chancel, Wormington, Glos. Bed scene approx. 21 inches square.

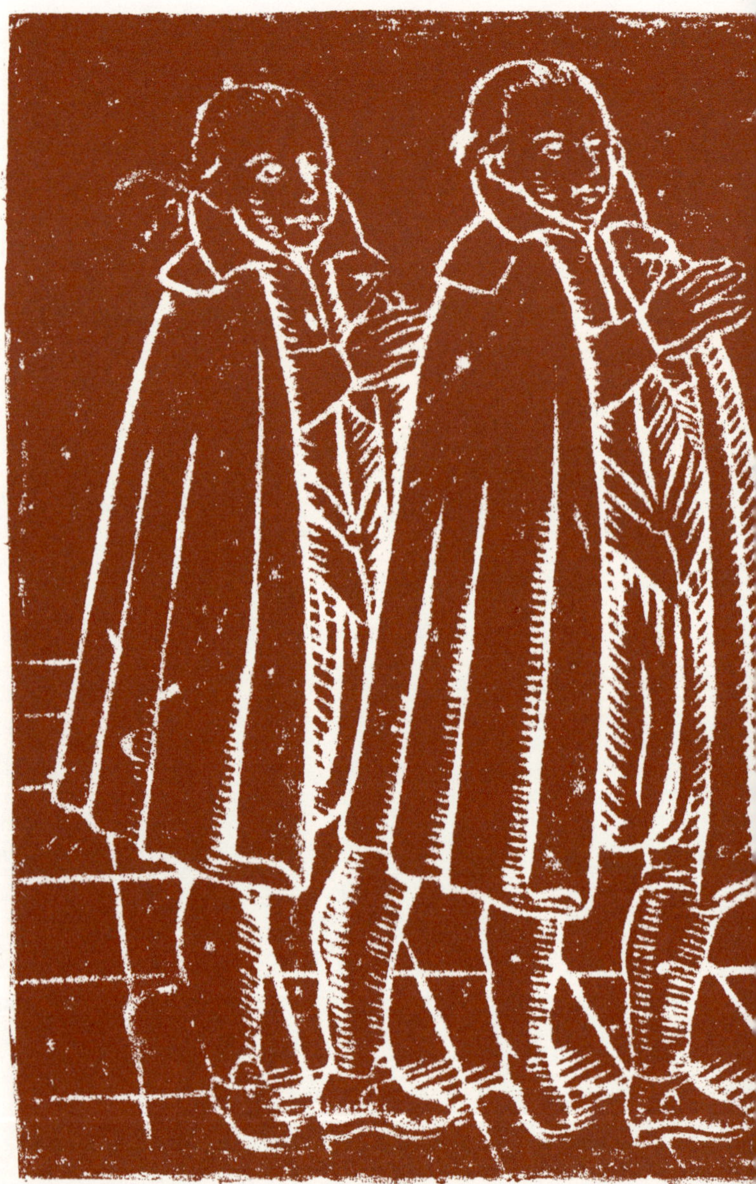

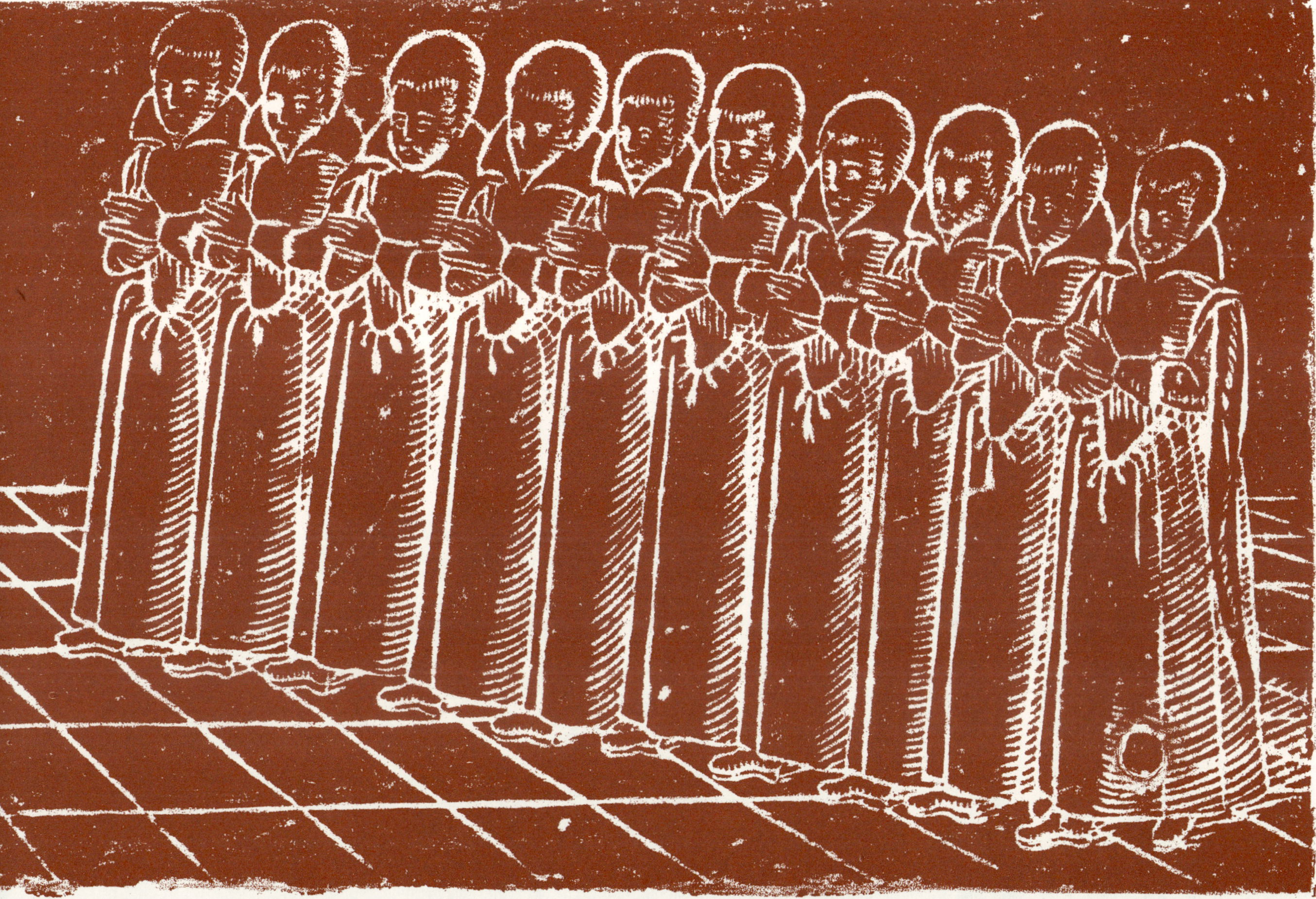

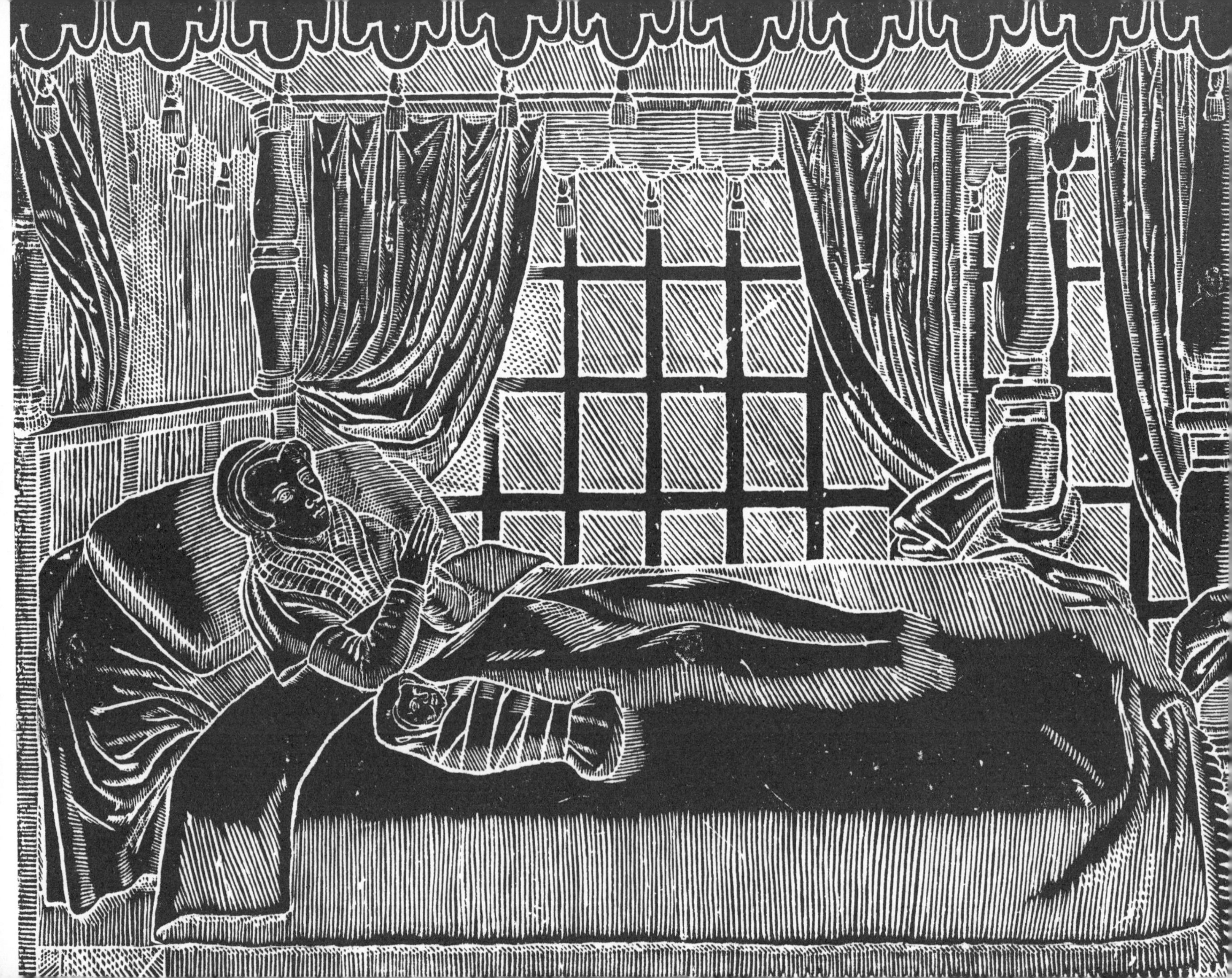

53, left

54, right

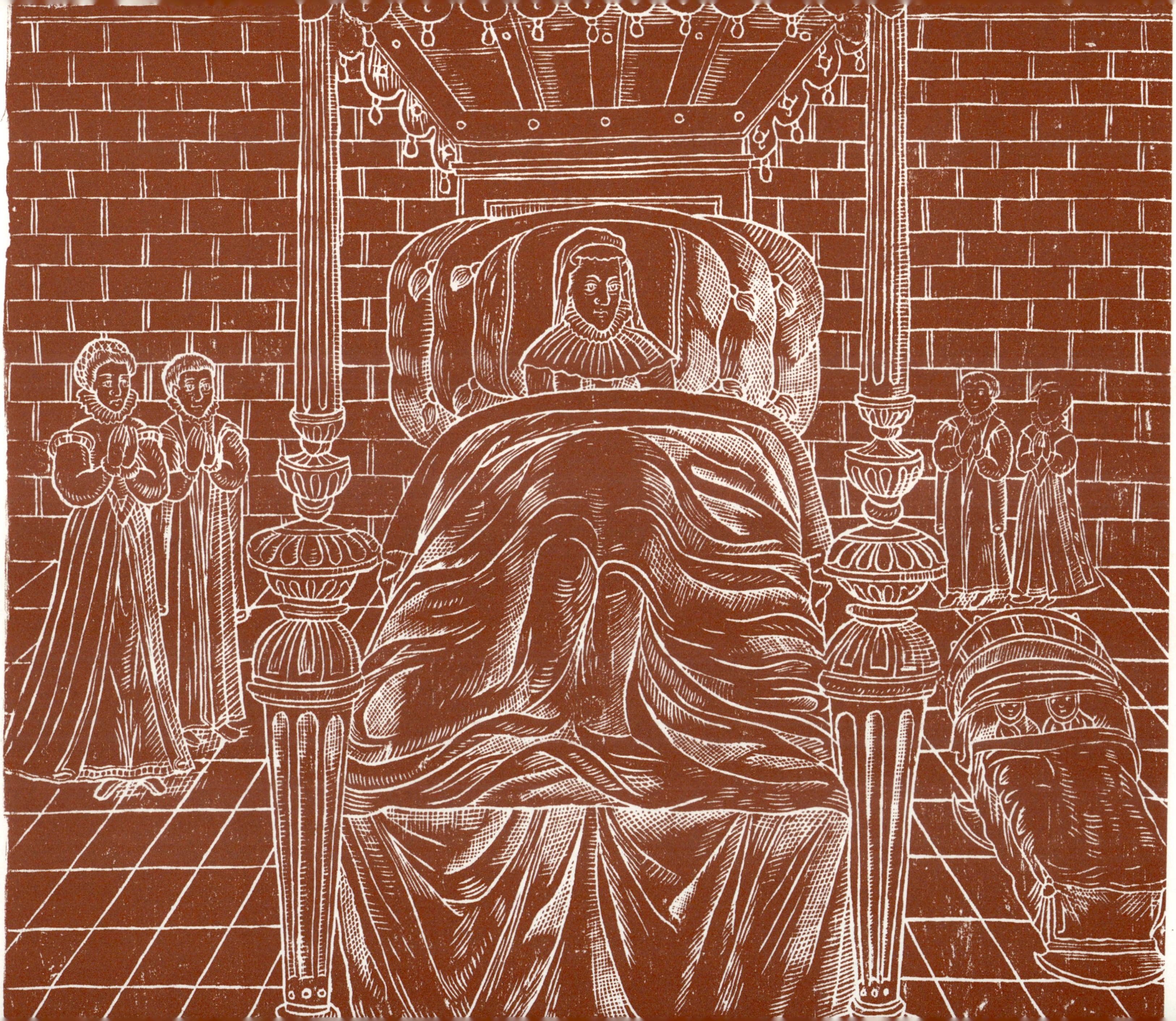

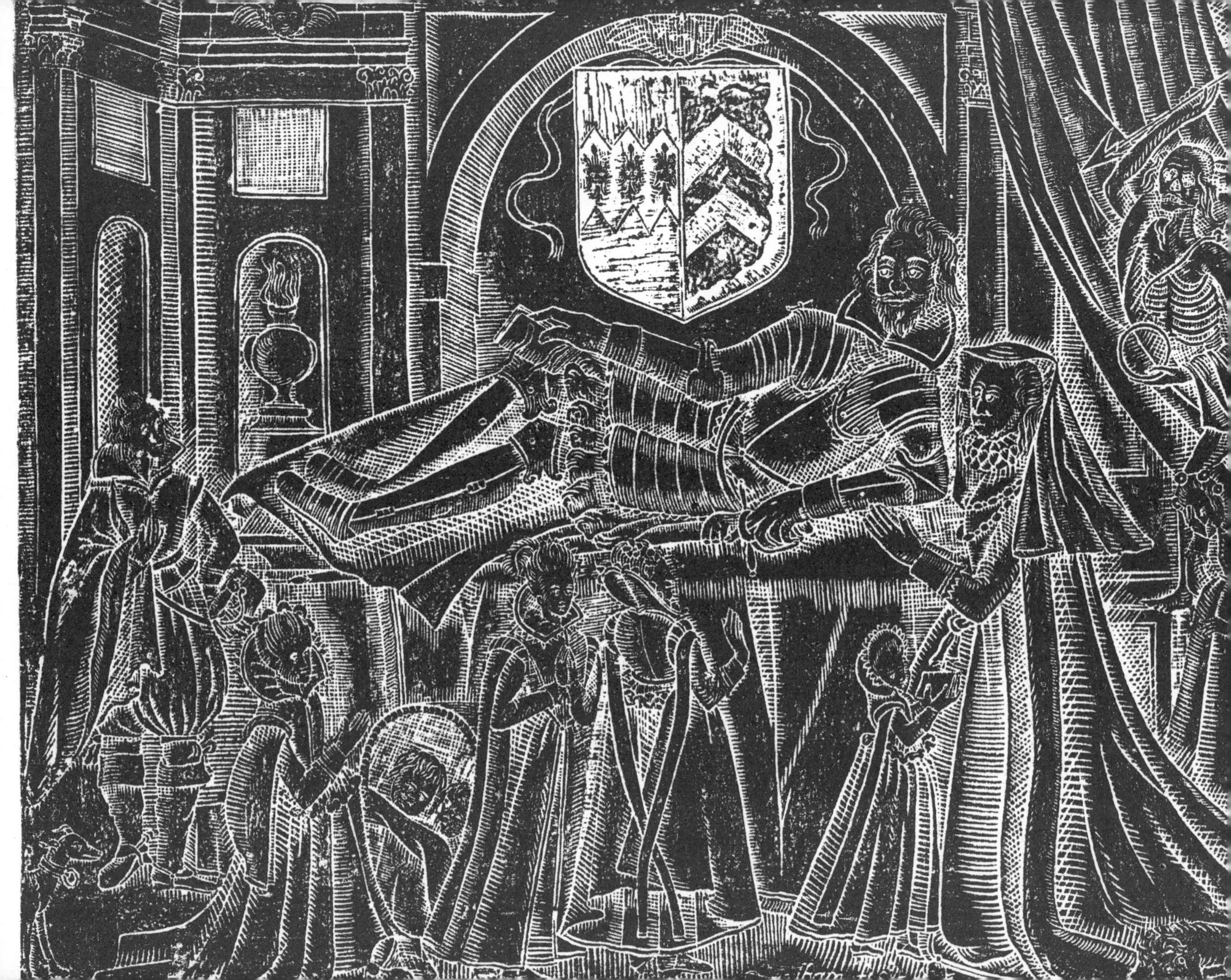

. 54, *reverse of facing page*

vester (1554–87) is propped up on a bolster and pillows in a four-poster bed. : died giving birth to twin sons Gore and Fane, shown in the cradle, who later ced the brass '*Gemelliparae positum*'. Two children by her first marriage stand her right, two other children, Multon and Margaret, by her second husband lliam Lambarde (1536–1601), stand behind the cradle. Lambarde published ious books including *A Perambulation of Kent* in 1576, which is the first nty history. In his will he left his daughter Margaret £800 for her marriage day 'together with my beste bedsteede and furniture therunto of silks and two of my best fetherbeddes, blankets, boulsters, and pillowes . . . and all such percells of beddinge lynnen and other aray therein used by her good mother my late godlie wyfe Silvester about her childberthe . . .'. Margaret married Thomas Godfrey. The brass is difficult to rub as it is recessed in a stone frame above the pulpit in Halling, Kent. Size approx. 19 inches square.

. 55, *facing*

ward West (d. 1618) reclines on his deathbed, one hand ding a book, and the other his sword, while Death creeps in hurl his arrow. Edmund's wife Theodosia and his eight ldren are grouped informally round him. There are two oies in a cradle and dogs in either corner. This highly ificial scene is interpreted in a naturalistic manner by iphamius Evesham, a sculptor who signs the plate. On end ak of an altar tomb, south chancel, Marsworth, Bucks. e $18\frac{1}{2}$ by $14\frac{3}{4}$ inches.

ield bears *arg. on a fess dancetty sa. 3 leopards heads ant-de-lys or.* for West, impaling *arg. 2 chevrons az. a dure engrailed gu.* for Tyrell.)

Fig. 56, below

William Hyde (d. 1614) in a cradle, 'being but an infant'. Little Ilford, Church Road, London E.12. Engraved *c.* 1630, on wall of nave. Same scale.

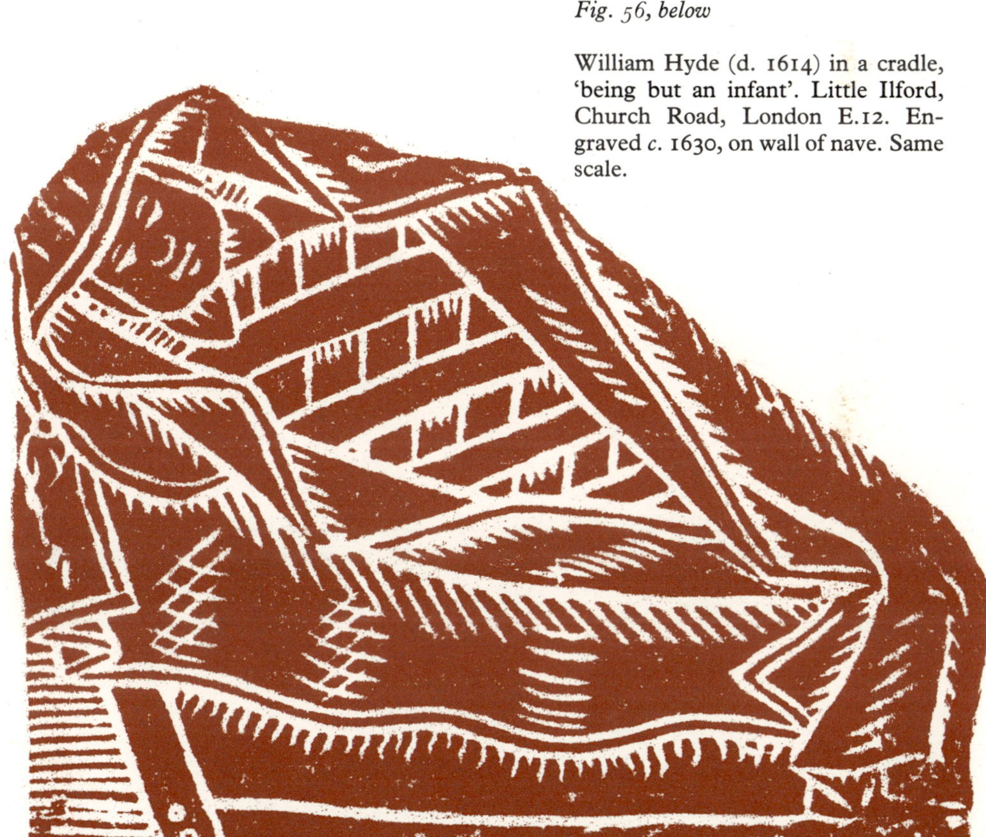

Fig. 57, below

Dorothy (d. 1630) was daughter of John King, who became Canon of Windsor in 1625 and lived until 1639. He published Latin orations and poems and may have supplied the engraver with the inscription and verse which have something of the metaphysical conceits of John Donne. Width of cradle 11½ inches.

'Dorothe King lent to her parents John King Dr of Divinitie
Praebendarie of this chappell and Marie his wife, but speedile requir'd againe Octobr. 18.16

Here lyes a modell of frail man
A tender infant; but a span
In age or stature; here shee must
Lengthen out both, bedded in dust
Nine moneths imprison'd in ye wombe;
Eight in earths surface free, ye tombe
Must make compleat hir diarie,
So leave hir to Aeternitie.'

The sensitive portrayal of children in Figs 57–60 may all be work of a sculptor, Edward Marshall, 1598–1675, who sig his work on a brass of 1629 at East Sutton, Kent.

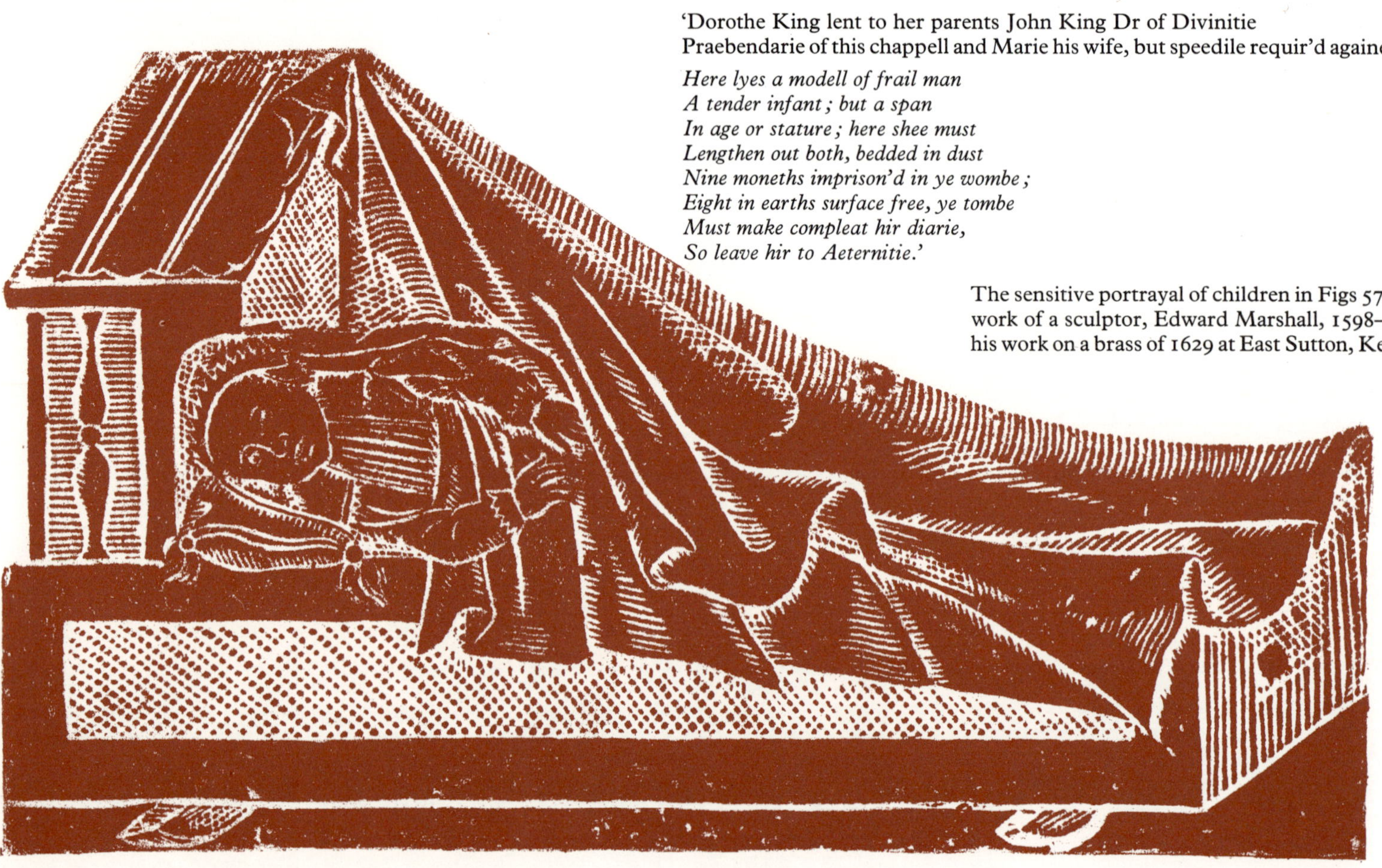

Fig. 58, right

At Wooburn, Bucks., Arthur, a nine-month-old son of Philip Lord Wharton (d. 1642) is drawn on his tomb holding a rose. On floor of chancel. Size 15 by 16½ inches.

59, right

Ienfield, Sussex, a nine-year-old boy Menelib Rainsford (d. 1627) stands beside his dmother, Mrs Anne Kenwellmersh (d. 1633) hat in hand. On floor of south chancel. ;ht $20\frac{1}{2}$ inches.

58

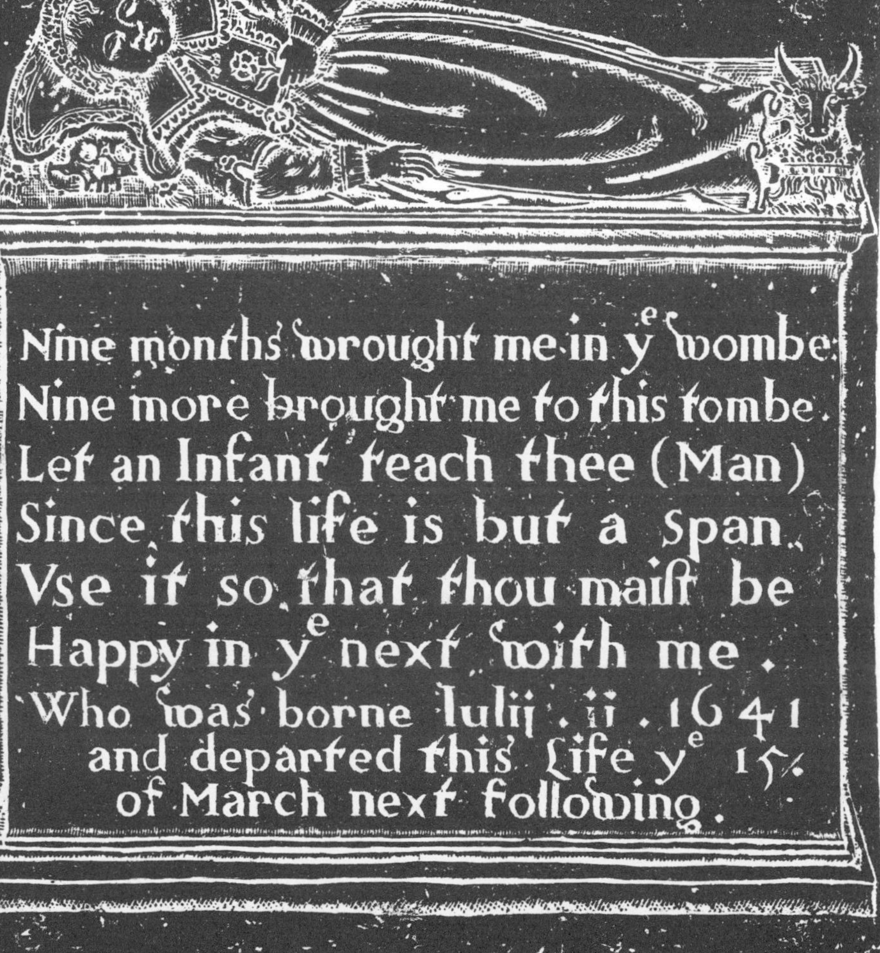

Fig. 59

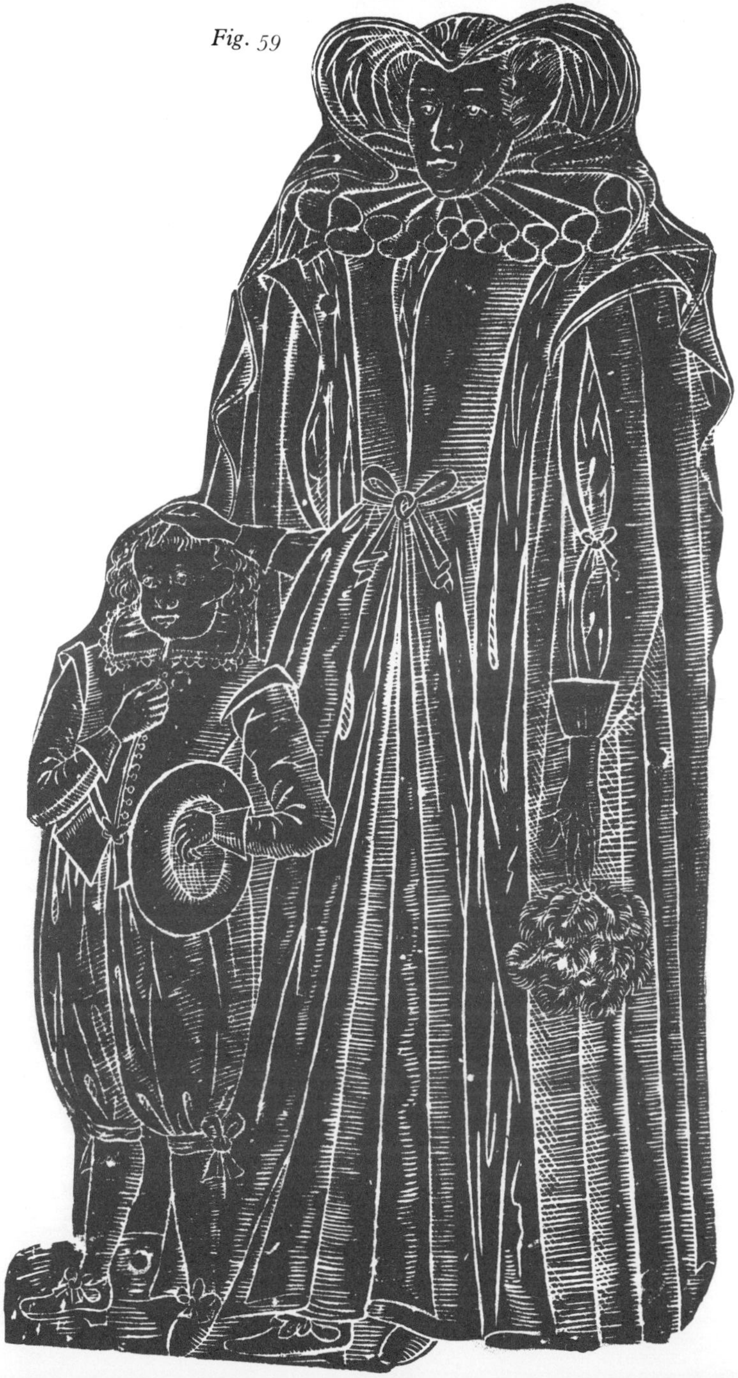

Fig. 60, below

'William King, second son to John King, Praebendarie of this chapple and Marie his wife being soone wearie of his abode on earth left them to praeserve a memoriall of him after ten weekes pilgrimage, under this marble 10 ber 22 1633.

Here the sad parents second sumons lyes
Withdrawn, to draw from earth to Paradise
Their stooping thoughts. Here hasten'd to repay
What they could lend, dull, macerated clay
To feast the wormes; what Heaven gave theire doth rest
To feast with innocents, thus from the brest,
Ravish't by Death, so nere our Saviours Birth
To share in Saints and Angels Christmas mirth.'

St Georges Chapel, Windsor, on floor of side chapel. Width of cradle 12½ inches.

Fig. 61, right

The vogue for memorial pictures in the early seventeenth century could have influence designers of brasses. Subjects for memorial pictures included swaddled babies and la death-bed compositions like this of Sir Thomas Aston beside his wife who died in childbir 1635. The black-draped wicker cradle bears a skull with the label *'Qui spem carne sem metet ossa'* (He who sows hope in the flesh reaps bones). His wife appears twice, lying de the bed and alluringly alive at the foot of the bed. Her son Thomas, aged 3 years 9 mo helps his father to hold a cross staff, a navigational instrument, and points to the inscri *'Numerantur astra mare novit similes'*. A celestial globe and unstrung lute rest on a leng exotic Indian cloth bearing elephants, lovers and the chase. We infer that although he name the stars and chart the seas he cannot measure his grief. Without his wife whc silent like an unstrung lute (see how beautiful she was) he is unbalanced. (Two years Thomas was dead and his father had married again.) The picture, painted by John Sou Chester, hangs in the City Art Gallery, Mosley Street, Manchester 2. Width 84½ inches

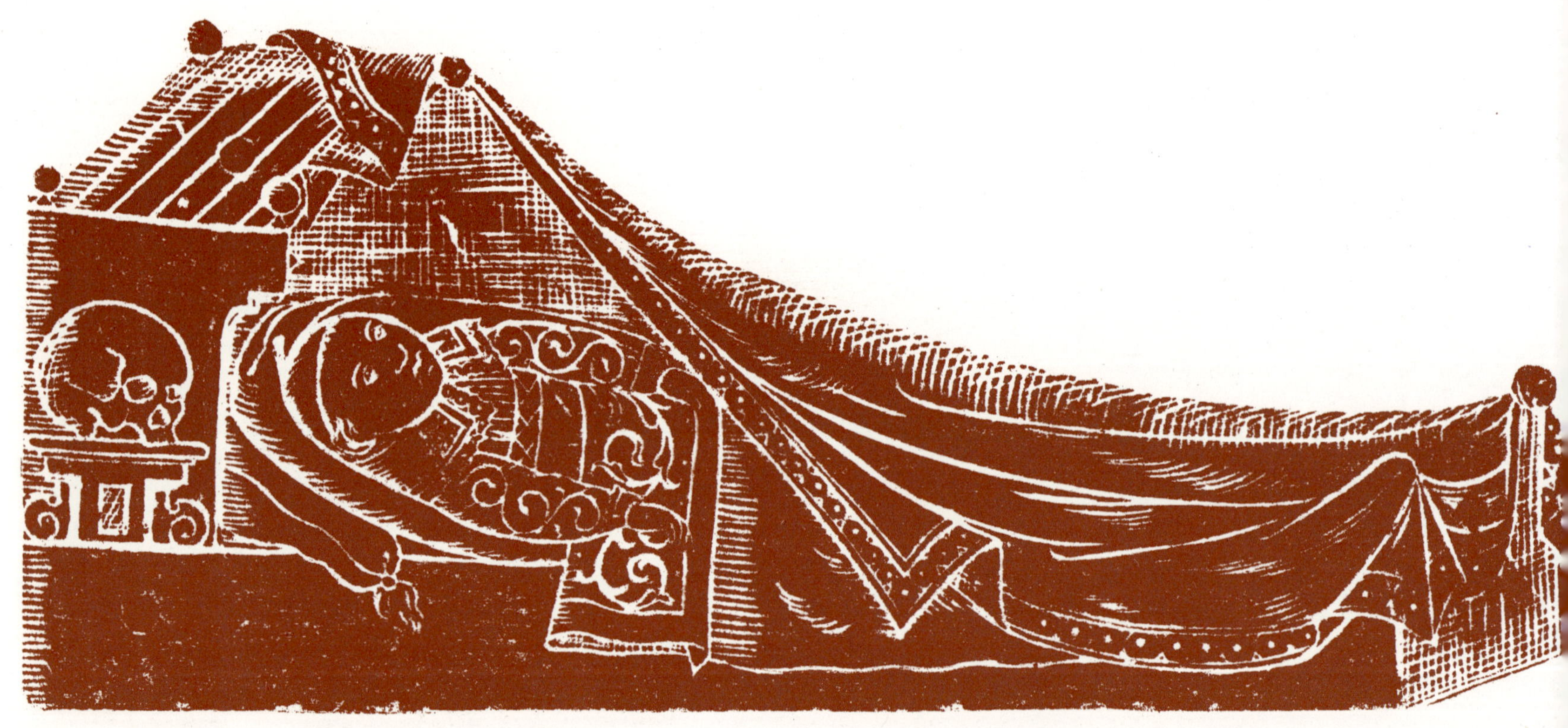

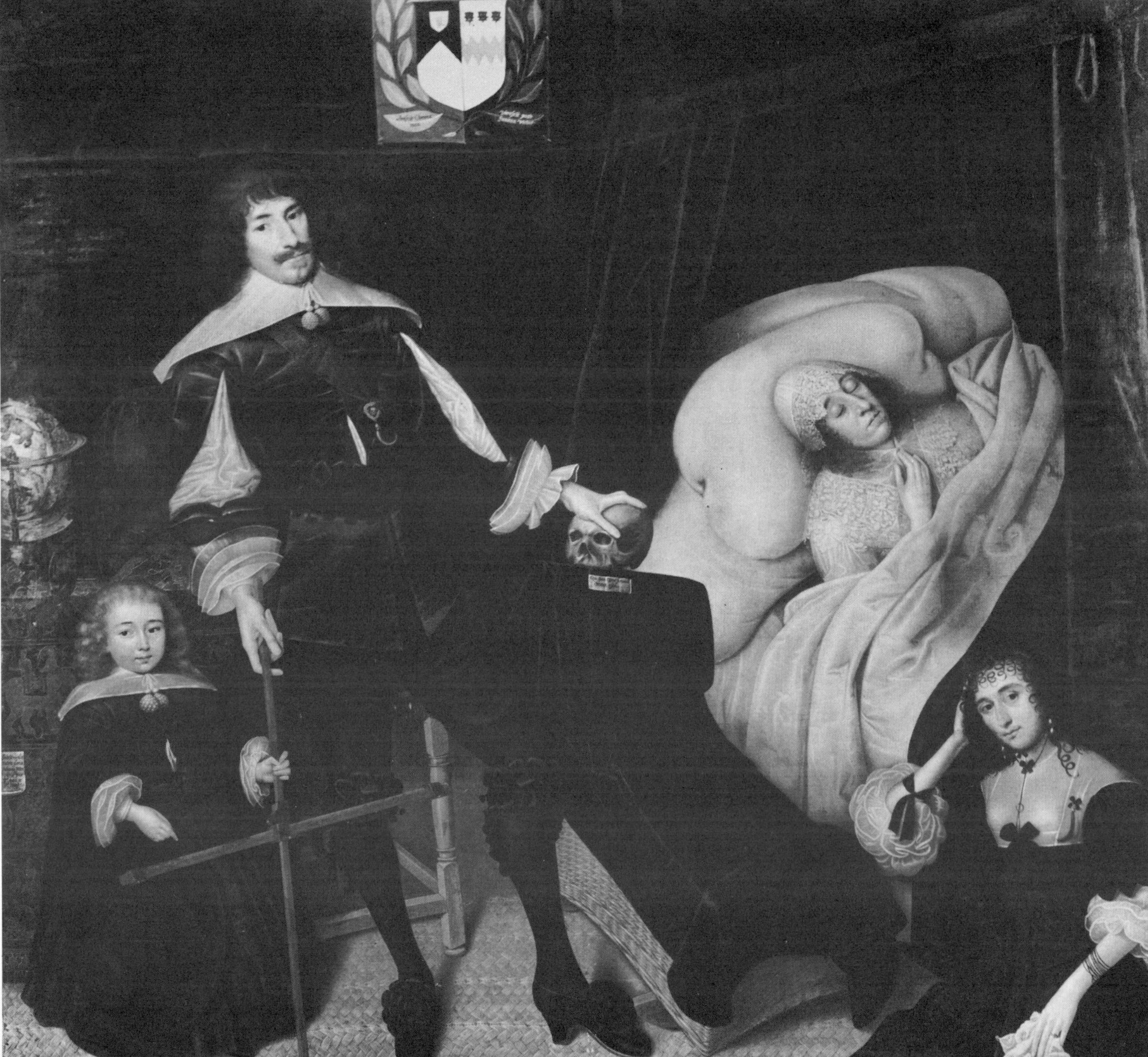

Fig. 62

Only hair tells the sons from the daughters of Richard Cheverton (d. 1617) and his wife Isabel (d. 1631). Probably designed in the West Country. On wall of south transept, Quethioc, Cornwall. Width 15½ inches.

Fig. 63, facing

Three kneeling daughters. Their father was Nicholas Toke (d. 1680), Great Chart, Kent. On floor of north chancel. Width 15½ inches. See p. 17.

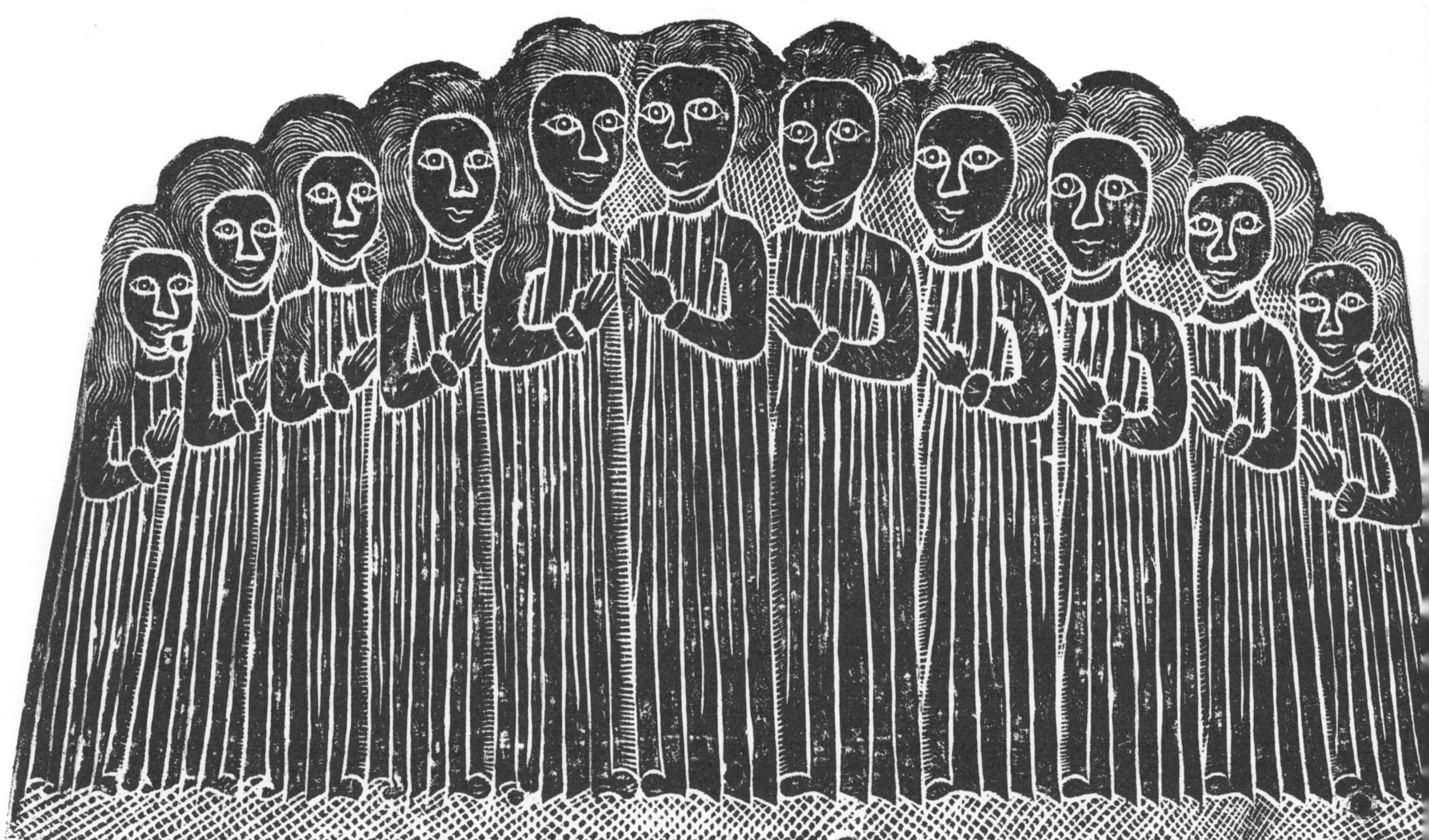

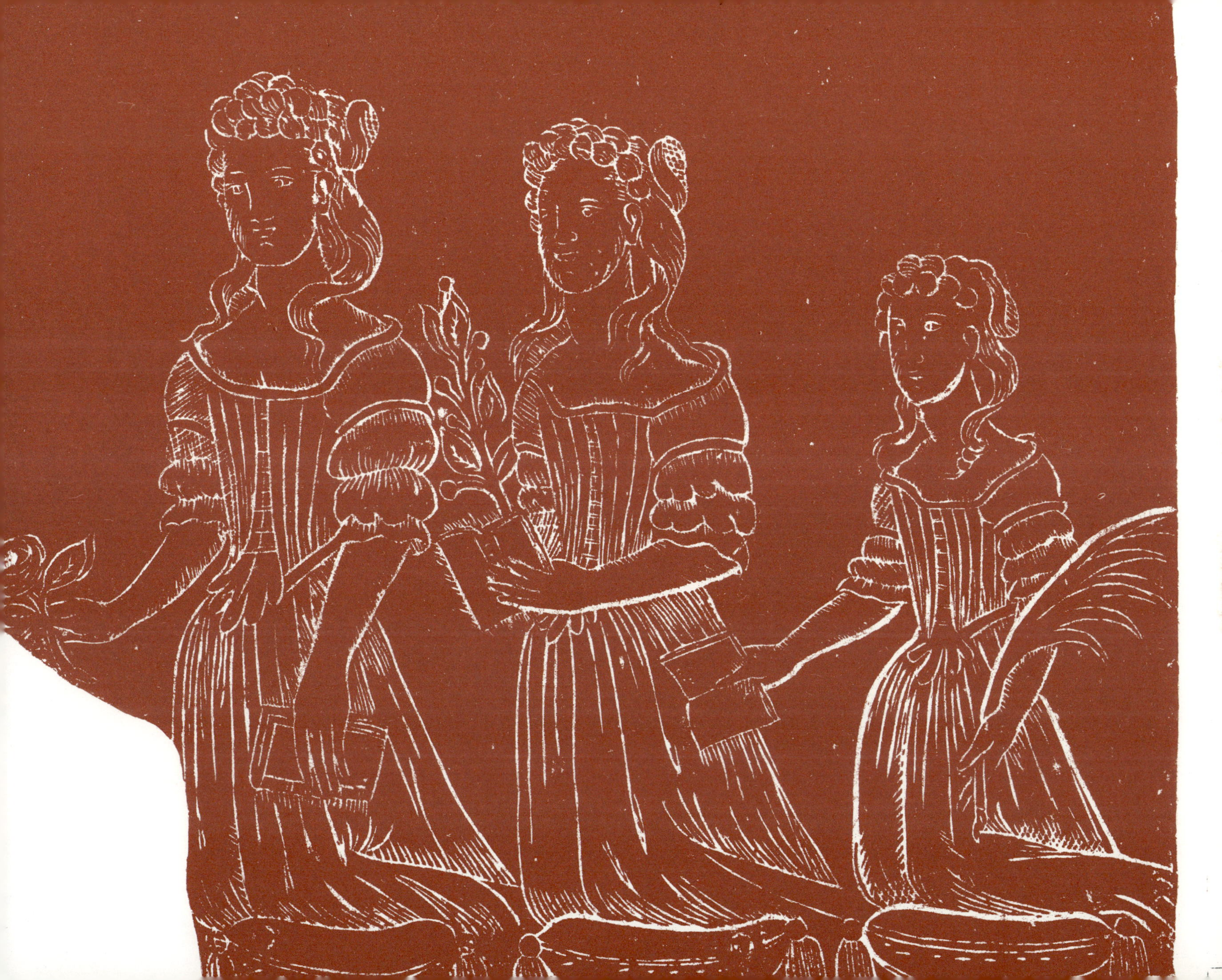

5. Selective Chronological List of 'Children on their Own Brasses'

N.R. means 'no rubbing allowed'

Fig.		*Date*	
	N.R.	1276	Westminster Abbey, London. Margaret de Valence, cross and Lombardic inscr. covered over, and
	N.R.	1277	Ditto William de Valence. These brasses are to the children of William de Valence, Henry III's half brother, and are included in the list because they are to children and the earlier is the oldest surviving brass in England.
1	N.R.	*c.* 1360	Sherborne St John, Hants. Half effigies of brother and sister.
2		1388	Great Marlow, Bucks. Lost brass showing four kneeling sons. Rubbings survive in Soc. Ant. and British Museum.
8		1414	Beddington, Surrey. Lady with her seven brothers and six sisters shown as a frieze of heads and shoulders.
16		1434	Headbourne Worthy, Hants. Winchester scholar.
		1455	Taplow, Bucks. Brother aged nineteen and maiden sister.
		1480	Etchingham, Sussex. Two girls with long hair, one has it plaited.
35		1505	Ditchingham, Norfolk. Brass to both father and son.
29		1510	Rougham, Norfolk. Two swaddled babies under tiny canopy.
18		1512	Wraysbury, Bucks. Possibly an Eton scholar.
	N.R.	1516	Stoke d'Abernon, Surrey. Chrysom.
17		1517	St Mary, Little Ilford, Church Road, London E.12. Schoolboy with pen case and ink pot.
		c. 1520	Chesham Bois, Bucks. Chrysom.
		c. 1520	Hornsey, Middx. Chrysom.
36		1525	Yelverton, Norfolk. Girl.
		1545	Denham, Bucks. Girl.
37 & 38		1551	Greystoke, Cumberland. Boy and girl.
45 & 48		1587	Merstham, Surrey. Boy and swaddled baby (baby renewed 1911).
46 & 47		1588	Aveley, Essex. Boy and girl.
49		1599	Holton, Oxon. Boy.
		1606	Boxford, Suffolk. Baby in cot.
		1611	Oxted, Surrey. Boy (head lost) and boy.
50		1623	Amersham, Bucks. Boy.
51		1629	Llandinabo, Herefordshire, Wales. Boy in pond in which he drowned.
56		*c.* 1630	St Mary, Little Ilford, Church Road, London, E.12. Baby in cradle.
57 & 60	N.R.	1630 1633	St George's Chapel, Windsor, Berks. Two brasses each showing a baby in a cradle.
		1633	Clynnog, Caernarvon, Wales. Boy.
		1634	Ardingley, Sussex. Girl.
		1636	Headcorn, Kent. Boy.
58	N.R.	1642	Wooburn, Bucks. Boy lying on tomb holding flower.

6. Selective Chronological List of 'Children on their Parents' Brasses'

No. of sons (M) and daughters (F)

N.R. means 'no rubbing allowed'

Fig.		*Date*	
4		1391	Stoke Fleming, Devon. Civilian with his granddaughter on a pedestal.
6		1397	Westminster Abbey. Thomas of Woodstock. All except slab lost, but drawing in Sandford's *Genealogical History*, 1677, shows children, 2 M on pedestals.
5		1405	Cobham, Kent. 2 M on pedestal (1 restored).
		1407	Cobham, Kent. 1 M on pedestal.
9		1415	Sudborough, Northants. 7 M (1 priest) 4 F.
		c. 1415	Luton, Beds. 1 M (1 priest, head repaired).
Back cover		1416	Ashby St Ledger, Northants. 4 M, 12 F.
7		1419	Linwood, Lincs. 4 M (1 priest), 3 F. In arcading.
	N.R.	1421	Trotton, Sussex. 1 M. Superimposed on folds of mother's dress.
	N.R.	1429	Newcastle-on-Tyne, Durham. 7 M, 7 F. Flemish.
11		1433	Cobham, Kent. 6 M, 4 F.
		1439	Brightwell Baldwin, Oxon. 5 M, 13 F. Kneeling.
12		1454	Blickling, Norfolk. 11 M, 5 F. Standing before their parents.
		1455	Broome, Norfolk. Children in shrouds.
13		1460	Stow-cum-Quy, Cambs. 12 M (in tabards), 4 F.
20		*c.* 1460	Elmdon, Essex. M lost, but once 4 M (1 abbot), 4 F. Formerly in Wendon Lofts.
		1467	Tong, Salop. 7 M, 5 F (2 lost).
		1467	Sawley, Derbyshire. 8 M (1 priest), 11 F.
14		1471	Quethioc, Cornwall. 11 M (1 priest, 1 yeoman of crown), 5 F.
15		1472	Thornton, Bucks. 3 wives. 3 M, 5 F; 2 M, 3 F; 1 M, 2 F.
		1478	Sawley, Derbyshire. M groups lost. 6 F.
	N.R.	1479	Dagenham, Essex. 4 M lost, 9 F (1 nun).
		c. 1480	Chelsfield, Kent. 6 M (2 priests), 5 F. With a tree between the sexes.
Frontis	N.R.	*c.* 1480	Peterborough Museum, Northants. 1 M, 1 F. On one plate.
19		1483	Stoke Charity, Hants. 2 M, 6 F.
21		1487	Oakley, Hants. 4 M (1 priest).
10		1487	Hinxworth, Herts. 4 M (1 priest), 2 F.
23		1488	Harrow, Middx. 3 wives. 1 priest; 5 M, 6 F; 2 M.
24		1489	Hornby, Yorks. 8 M (3 in armour, 1 priest), 7 F (1 nun).

Fig.		*Date*	
		c. 1490	Ealing St Mary, London. 3 M, 6 F. Kneeling with parents.
		1496	Hutton, Somerset. 4 M, 7 F.
		c. 1490	Orford, Suffolk. 3 M, 7 F. At feet of mother.
26		1500	Wrotham, Kent. 5 F. Kneeling.
25		1500	Longworth, Berks. 5 M (3 in shrouds) worn, 8 F (4 in shrouds).
27		1501	Lacock, Wilts. 13 M (1 priest), 5 F.
		1502	Thame, Oxon. 2 wives. 5 M lost, 8 F; 7 M, 5 F.
28		1503	Great Coates, Lincs. 8 M (1 priest), 7 F (1 nun). Ranged behind kneeling parents.
		1505	Impington, Cambs. 7 M, 2 F.
		1506	Leckhampstead, Bucks. 3 F.
30		1509	Teynham, Kent. 1 swaddled baby and 1 F on one plate.
		1512	Etwall, Derbyshire. 9 M, 8 F.
		1512	Cobham, Kent. 8 M, 10 F. On one plate.
31		1512	Blickling, Norfolk. Mother holding twin swaddled babies.
33		*c.* 1515	Minchinhampton, Glos. 6 M (1 monk), 3 F (1 nun).
		1515	Whalley, Lancs. 9 M (1 priest), 11 F.
		c. 1520	Aldenham, Herts. 2 M (5 feet!), 6 F.
		c. 1520	Cranbrook, Kent. 1 swaddled baby.
34	N.R.	*c.* 1520	Burnham, Bucks. 9 M (lost), 15 F.
		c. 1520	Worlingworth, Suffolk. 4 M (1 priest), 7 F.
		1526	Compton Verney, Warwicks. 9 M, 5 F.
		c. 1530	Beaumaris, Anglesey, Wales. 2 M (1 priest), 1 F. Kneeling behind parents.
39		1534	Radnage, Bucks. 8 M (1 priest), 5 F.

Fig.		*Date*	
40		1538	Norbury, Derbyshire. 5 F (eldest in heraldic mantle).
42	N.R.	1538	Okeover, Staffs. 8 M, 5 F. Grotesquely placed on rev. of *c.* 1450 lady. Mutilated and broken in many pieces.
		1547	Aldbury, Herts. 9 M, 3 F.
41		*c.* 1550	Margaretting, Essex. 3 M, 4 F.
44		1551	St Mellion, Cornwall. 17 M, 7 F.
		1554	Ludford, Herefordshire. 9 M, 6 F (1 lost).
		1572	Colan, Cornwall. 13 M, 9 F. On rectangular plate with parents.
		1574	Constantine, Cornwall. 8 M, 8 F.
		1575	Whitchurch, Denbigh, Wales. 9 M, 7 F. Kneeling with parents.
		1578	Bromham, Wilts. 1 M, 2 F (1 lost). Kneeling with parents.
		c. 1580	Wendron, Cornwall. 8 M, 8 F.
		1580	Newington, Kent. 2 M. Standing beside mother who has hand on head of one.
Front cover		1581	Dartford, Kent. Mother holding swaddled baby.
		1587	Thames Ditton, Surrey. 14 M, 5 F. Kneeling with parents.
54		1587	Lower Halling, Kent. Mother on deathbed, with her children, 2 as babies, sharing a cradle.
32		1592	Haughton-le-Skerne, Durham. Mother holding twin babies.
53		1605	Wormington, Glos. Mother on deathbed with swaddled baby.
52		1611	Wrotham, Kent. 2 M, 10 F. On one plate.
55		1618	Marsworth, Bucks. Unusual design of son, daughter and cradle grouped round

Fig.	Date	
		father's deathbed on which he reclines in armour. Signed by Evesham.
	1622	St Cross, Holywell, Oxford. Mother on deathbed with three shrouds and one swaddled baby.
	1629	East Sutton, Kent. 9 M, 9 F. Signed by Ed. Marshall.
62	1631	Quethioc, Cornwall. 11 children. Part of quaintly drawn brass.
59	1633	Henfield, Sussex. Lady with *grandson*.
	1636	Edwardstone, Suffolk. 6 M, 6 F.
	1640	St Sepulchre, Northampton, Northants. 2 wives. 2 M, 1 F; 7 M, 2 F.
	1641	Penn, Bucks. 5 M, 5 F.
	1657	Sheriff Hutton, Yorks. Mother holding swaddled baby.
63	1680	Great Chart, Kent. 3 F.

7. The Selective Lists Arranged by Counties

Dates in Italics show 'Children on their own Brasses'

Bedfordshire
Cople 1544
Luton *c.* 1415

Berkshire
Hurst *c.* 1600
Longworth 1509
St George's Chapel, Windsor *1630*, *1633* N.R.

Buckinghamshire
Amersham *1623*
Burnham *c.* *1520* (part lost)
Chesham Bois *c.* 1520
Denham *1545*
Leckhampstead 1506
Marlow, Great *1388* (lost)
Marsworth 1618
Penn 1641
Radnage 1534
Taplow *1455*
Thornton 1472
Wooburn *1642* N.R.
Wraysbury *1512*

Cambridgeshire
Impington 1505
Stow-cum-Quy 1460

Cornwall
Colan 1572
Constantine 1574
Quethioc 1471, 1631
St Mellion 1551
Wendron *c.* 1580

Cumberland
Greystoke *1551*

Derbyshire
Etwall 1512
Norbury 1538
Sawley 1467, 1478

Devon
Stoke Fleming 1391 (civilian and granddaughter)

Durham
Haughton-le-Skerne 1592
Newcastle-on-Tyne 1429 N.R.

Essex
Aveley *1588*
Dagenham 1479 N.R.
Elmdon *c.* 1460 (part lost; formerly in Wendon Lofts.)
Little Ilford *1517*
Margaretting *c.* 1559

Gloucestershire
Minchinhampton *c.* 1510
Wormington 1605

Hampshire
Headbourne Worthy *1434*
Oakley 1487
Sherborne St John *c. 1360* N.R.
Stoke Charity 1483

Herefordshire
Llandinabo *1629*
Ludford 1554

Hertfordshire
Aldbury 1547
Aldenham *c.* 1520
Hinxworth 1487

Kent
Chart, Great 1680
Chelsfield *c.* 1480
Cobham 1405, 1407, 1433, 1512
Cranbrook *c.* 1520
Dartford 1581
Halling, Lower 1587
Headcorn *1636*
Newington 1580
Sutton, East 1629
Teynham 1509
Wrotham 1611

Lancashire
Whalley 1515

Lincolnshire
Coates, Great 1503
Linwood 1419

Middlesex
Harrow 1488
Heston 1581 N.R. (under fixed carpeting)
Hornsey *c. 1520*

London, Ealing St Mary *c.* 1490
London, Westminster Abbey *1276*, *1277* (both covered), 1397 (lost) N.R.

Norfolk
Blickling 1454, 1512
Broome 1455
Ditchingham *1505*
Ketteringham 1499
Rougham *1510*
Yelverton *1525*

Northamptonshire
Ashby St Ledger 1416
Northampton, St Sepulchre 1640
Peterborough Museum *c.* 1480 N.R.
Sudborough 1415

Oxfordshire
Brightwell Baldwin 1439
Holton *1599*
Oxford, Holywell St Cross 1622
Thame 1502

Shropshire
Tong 1467

Somerset
Hutton 1496

Staffordshire
Okeover 1538 N.R.

Suffolk
Boxford *1606*
Edwardstone 1636
Orford *c.* 1490
Worlingworth *c.* 1520

Surrey
Beddington *1414*
Merstham *1587*
Oxted *1611*
Stoke d'Abernon *1516* N.R.
Thames Ditton 1587

Sussex
Ardingley *1634*
Etchingham *1480*
Henfield 1633
Trotton 1421 N.R.

Warwickshire
Compton Verney 1526

Wiltshire
Bromham 1578
Lacock 1501

Yorkshire
Hornby 1489
Sheriff Hutton 1657

Wales
Beaumaris, Anglesey *c.* 1530
Clynnog, Caernarvon *1633*
Whitchurch, Denbighshire 1575